SONOITA PLAIN

Views from a Southwestern Grassland

Text by

CARL E. BOCK *and* JANE H. BOCK

Photographs by STEPHEN E. STROM
Foreword by PATRICIA NELSON LIMERICK

THE UNIVERSITY OF ARIZONA PRESS

Tucson

Frontispiece: Topographic map of the Sonoita Valley area.

The University of Arizona Press
Text ©2005 Carl E. Bock and Jane H. Bock
Photos ©2005 Stephen Strom (except for the rattlesnake photo on page 56)
⊚This book is printed on acid-free, archival-quality paper.
Manufactured in China

10   09   08   07   06   05   6   5   4   3   2   1

Library of Congress Cataloging-in-Publication Data

Bock, Carl E., 1942–
Sonoita Plain : views from a Southwestern grassland / text by Carl E. Bock and Jane H. Bock ;
photographs by Stephen Strom ; foreword by Patricia Nelson Limerick.
      p. cm.
Includes bibliographical references.
      ISBN 0-8165-2362-2 (pbk. : alk. paper)
      ISBN 0-8165-2363-0 (cloth : alk. paper)
      1. Grassland ecology—Arizona—Santa Cruz County. 2. Santa Cruz county (Ariz.)—History.
I. Bock, Jane H. II. Title.
QH105.A4B63 2005
577.4′09791′79—dc22
2004008494

CONTENTS

ILLUSTRATIONS

SOME WESTERN RODEOS include an event called the mule pull, an event that makes up in psychological interest what it lacks in wild action. Two mules are harnessed together and encouraged to pull a weight placed on a sledge that rests flat on the ground. The mules are perfectly capable of pulling the weight *if*—and this is a very big *if*—they will consent to the project of pulling together, at the same time and in the same direction. Being mules, their response to common, coordinated enterprise is often an operating definition of the term *reluctance.* It is a great temptation to them to dismiss the project of pulling the weight and to put their attention and energy into trying to bite their partner's nose instead.

Rather in the spirit of the mule pull, Jane Bock, Carl Bock, and Stephen Strom undertake in this book to persuade Ecology and Aesthetics to go into harness together and to encourage them to pull together in the same direction, at the same time. This is not an easy task, because thousands and thousands of human beings have devoted enormous time and effort to dividing, separating, and segregating "science" from "art," casting them, at best, as unrelated human enterprises and, at worst, as opposite and conflicting forces. And there is the added problem that Aesthetics seems to have pulled far ahead of Ecology in the race for the public's good opinion and support, if not in the race for federal funding. If someone breaks into a museum and damages or defaces a work of art, every citizen is outraged, and the criminal, if discovered, will face disapprobation, prosecution, and very probably a life within the limited "viewscape" of prison. But if someone builds and occupies a house in sensitive wildlife habitat and thereby damages or defaces the existing ecology, reducing the numbers of an already endangered species, a few environmentalists may condemn the house's impact, but its owner and occupant will probably live happily ever after, pleased with his circumstances and happy with the expansive view from his picture window.

It is not easy being a lover of fine art in a world in which the Philistines seem to rule. Yet it is even harder being a connoisseur of fine nature in a world in which the oblivious call the shots.

So Aesthetics may seem to have outdistanced Ecology, making the project of persuading them to join in the same enterprise look like a tough one. And yet a deeper perspective over time might suggest that the separation in popular opinion of Aesthetics from Ecology is, actually, a rather recent misfortune, and a remediable one at that. Two hundred years ago, the Romantic Movement merged and melded aesthetic response to nature with aesthetic response to human-created art, and it seems very tenable to argue that this merging has been more the rule than the exception in human societies. Separating the category "art" from the category "nature" was an unusual—and weird—accomplishment of comparatively recent times. In this context, by bringing Aesthetics and Ecology to bear on an appreciation of the Arizona grasslands, the authors of this book are arranging for something closer to a reunion of closely related values, rather than to the forging of a new relationship.

When I read the manuscript that would become this book, I was emphatically and certifiably *nowhere.* I was sitting in an airplane traveling between Chicago and Denver, and the only fauna available for my observation were wearing business attire and tapping at their laptops. And yet, even though the Sonoita Valley's agaves, snakes, jays, flickers, Botteri's sparrows, and antelope were operating at an enormous distance (both laterally and vertically!) from me, they were within my reach. Even in the ridiculously abstract territory of a plane 30,000 feet off the surface of the earth, I knew that, thanks to the human powers of observation and expression, I was "seeing" those entities with greater clarity, definition, and understanding than I could have mustered if my plane had suddenly been diverted to southern Arizona, landed on the road outside Elgin, extruded its evacuation slide, and allowed me to try to see these things for myself.

This feeling of immediacy was further enhanced by a tour through Stephen Strom's photographs. In the late nineteenth century, when photographers such as William Henry Jackson and Timothy Sullivan turned their attention to the West, their attention was drawn to the vast view and the sweeping landscape. It took some time—a century or so—for photographers working in the West to develop the courage to give up the expected "big picture" and to recognize that the West's natural beauty could be found at every scale. The devil may or may not be in the details, but the details also contain their fair share of magic, power, and glory. Strom's photographs direct our attention to the patterns and configurations that bind sky to earth, plant to water, animal to herd; and those recorded observations, like the writings of the Bocks, represent Ecology and Aesthetics pulling together—or, more accurately, dancing together.

Nineteenth-century Americans had a gift we have let slide. Once upon a time, there were hundreds and thousands of what we might call "masters of vicarious experience." Living before the automobiles and airplanes that have made us feel entitled to see everything for ourselves, these people of the past knew how to make the most of the testimony of their delegated agents.

Explorers traveled in the West; they recruited artists and photographers to travel with them; these teams made sketches, took notes, and exposed photographic plates; then they all came home and assembled their reports. Even though readers knew they would never visit the places described, or (more to the point) precisely *because* they knew they would never visit those places, readers absorbed these reports with intensity.

This was important as an aesthetic experience, but it was also significant as social policy. Much scorned in our times, "couch potatoes" offer one remedy for such problems as the excessive recreational use of some public lands. The Bocks generously offer suggestions to readers on how they might visit this wonderful part of North America. But my own invitation would be a bit different. First, do a historical reenactment of the nineteenth-century American's mastery of vicarious experience; sit on a couch and read this book with the intensity with which the text was written and the photographs were made. Second, take a vigorous walk around your neighborhood, and as you walk, apply the observational skills that the Bocks and Strom have modeled for you. Look at details of soil, flora, fauna, and landscape; look at the sky and how it meets the earth; look for connections: let Aesthetics and Ecology pull you along on your walk, and then go home, contented.

But do not, repeat, do not get so inspired that you decide you must build or buy a second home in the Sonoita Valley. This is my advice, not the Bocks' or Strom's. These are tolerant and good-natured people; while they are lovers of nature, they also have a pretty soft spot in their hearts for human beings. They portray the people of the Sonoita Valley with affection and respect. In an era when advocates for nature sometimes do convincing imitations of the most smug and self-righteous religious believers, condemning sin in others and ignoring it in themselves, the Bocks and Strom are a refreshing exception. "Human population growth in the Sonoita Valley," they acknowledge, ". . . is the fault of newcomers like Carl and Jane Bock, and Stephen and Karen Strom, deciding for very good reasons that this is a good place to live."

Rather than wasting their time, and their readers' time, in dreaming of a world in which nature does not have to put up with pesky human beings, these authors do not exalt the antelope over the coffee-shop waitresses, the flickers over the members of the Sonoita Crossroads Community Forum. Instead, they place human beings in the picture (and award them all of part three of this book) as subjects for the perspectives supplied by Aesthetics and Ecology.

Consider the term most commonly used for the nineteenth-century writers of reports on the West: *naturalist.* This was, and remains, a pretty good word. The "-ist" at the end claimed expertise, knowledge of nature. But that enterprising suffix carries other associations. As in *pianist* or *trombonist, naturalist* also conveys a capacity to play with and on the material of nature. And, of course, the suffix also suggests commitment to, and sometimes advocacy of, a cause, as in *abolitionist* or *suffragist* or, alas, *prohibitionist.*

In the comparatively recent onset of extreme specialization, as science divided itself up into increasingly tiny chunks of expertise, naturalists became an underrepresented species. This book is one particularly heartening example that they are coming back in force. And just in time: decisions made now and in the next few years will have enormous consequences in determining the range and diversity of species that humans in the future will have the opportunity to contemplate, study, appreciate, and admire.

The naturalists needed in the early twenty-first century must, however, also be humanists, in all senses of the suffix "-ist"— knowledgeable about humans, capable of playing with and on the material of human nature, and willing to speak out and press for the best interests of humans. The authors of this book show us how to be both naturalist and humanist: warning us, instructing us, amusing us, and raising our spirits at one and the same time.

ACKNOWLEDGMENTS

INDIVIDUALS AND ORGANIZATIONS almost too numerous to list have hosted our work in the Sonoita Valley over the past thirty years. First and foremost, we thank the National Audubon Society in general and the staff of the Appleton-Whittell Research Ranch Sanctuary in particular, including Bill Branan, Linda Kennedy, Sam Campana, and Frank Gill, both for providing the facilities and for nurturing the land and its living things, which are the subjects of our research and photographic efforts. Thanks also are due to two federal land management agencies, the U.S. Forest Service and Bureau of Land Management, that not only had the foresight to dedicate those public sections of the Research Ranch to the overall purposes of the sanctuary, but also hosted and supported much of our work elsewhere in the valley. Perhaps our greatest debt of gratitude goes to Frank and Ariel Appleton (and to their children, Bryce, Marc, Lee, and Lynn), who had the wisdom to conceive of the Research Ranch in the first place and then the generosity to support it by giving their land.

Next, we gratefully acknowledge the hospitality of owners and managers of three large ranches in the Sonoita Valley: Ben Brophy, Anne Gibson, and Doug Ruppel of the Babacomari Ranch, Rukin and Rukie Jelks and Joe Quiroga of the Diamond C Ranch, and John and Mac Donaldson of the Empire Ranch. You have been careful and caring stewards of the land and generously tolerant of our continual traipsing across it. No less patient and helpful have been many other residents of the valley and southern Arizona, and elsewhere, who have accommodated our fieldwork and helped in many other ways: Mary Bartol, Helen and Dan Beal, Sis and George Bradt, Jovana and Bill Brown, Gail and Bill Eifrig, Jane Church, Jacque and Shel Clark, Nancy and Bill Cook, James Curry, Sarah Dinham, Billie and Mac Donaldson, Barbara and John Donaldson, Mary Peace Douglas, Sidney Franklin, Leo Gonzales, Sally Greenleaf, Phil Heilman, Patricia and the late Fred Hoffman, Michael Johnson, Jim Kolbe, Shela McFarlin, Vista and John Michael, Mary Kay O'Rourke and Paul Martin, Dick Reilly, Susan Shields, Laurel Wilkening and Godfrey Sill, Dorothy Sturges, Molly and Doug Webster, Jane Woods, and Kazz and Pete Workizer.

Many individuals and organizations have supported our research in the Sonoita Valley, most recently the Arizona Game and Fish Department, the Research Ranch Foundation, and the National Science Foundation. The students, colleagues, and field assistants who have helped with our work are too numerous to list, but for recent help we particularly wish to thank Greg Joder, Brian Loomis, and Zach Jones.

Finally, we thank Patti Hartmann and her colleagues at the University of Arizona Press, especially Christine Szuter, Al Schroder, Nancy Arora, and Harrison Shaffer, and freelance editor Sally Bennett. This book would not have been possible without your insights, editorial skills, encouragement, and guidance.

SPECIAL THANKS

The University of Colorado

In memory of J. Frederick Hoffman
—Patricia Hoffman

From an admiring friend
—Mary Bartol

We're very proud to be involved with this book.
—John and Vista Michael

In memory of my mother, Ariel Bryce Appleton
—Marc Appleton

INTRODUCTION

MOST OF THE PLACES that humans have protected as treasured parks or wilderness are forests, tundras, wetlands, seashores, or deserts. It is in the grasslands that we have *lived,* and usually these places have been too useful to set aside. The plants and animals we have domesticated betray our history as the world's most important grassland animal. Our three most important foods are corn, wheat, and rice—all grasses. Our livestock hold grasslands hostage for their foodstuff. We live *in* grasslands, and we live *off* them. They are our backyards, in an evolutionary if no longer always in a literal sense.

Grasslands constitute nearly one-quarter of Earth's land surface. At the time of Columbus more than 900 million acres of grassland existed in North America, more than any other type of plant community. Since then nearly 60 percent of the grasslands in the United States have been lost to crop production and urbanization, and most of those remaining are dedicated to livestock grazing. Given the agricultural importance of grasslands, it is no surprise that humans have altered them more than any other of the world's great ecosystems. Nor is it surprising that our comparatively recent efforts at conservation have protected grasslands relatively poorly. And yet, what places deserve more protection as both genetic and environmental resources? From what places might we learn more about our own evolutionary roots than from grasslands preserved in something resembling their prehistoric condition?

In this book we introduce you by words and images to a small grassland in the Southwest whose conservation lies closest to our hearts. The Sonoita Valley of Santa Cruz County is a rolling savanna of grass and oak and mesquite in the high country of southeastern Arizona. Grasslands of the American Southwest are at once typical of and distinct from their widespread and relatively more familiar counterparts in the North American Great Plains. The same three environmental forces affecting prairies in Kansas or Saskatchewan or anywhere else in North America also determine their distribution and character in Arizona and New Mexico: drought, grazing by animals, and fire. The U.S.–Mexico borderlands once were the cradle from which many modern grass genera and species first appeared. These lands also were among the places where grassland plants and animals survived during the ice ages, when it was too cold and wet farther north. As a result, much of what we see in the plains and prairies of the rest of North America today had their origin in places similar to the Sonoita Valley, tens of thousands of years in the past.

In the modern era, grasslands of the Southwest have found themselves in a relatively precarious environmental position, squeezed into a narrow elevation belt between deserts below and woodlands above, and frequently invaded by trees and shrubs coming from both directions. Fossil evidence suggests that grasslands such as those of the Sonoita Valley have decreased and recovered numerous times through the ages, probably in response to subtle changes in climate. Lately, however, human activities have forced these changes largely in one direction—from grassland to woodland or desert scrub.

Across most of the central Great Plains, and even down into Chihuahua, the grasslands once were dominated by large herds of bison, North America's principal large grazing mammal. Yet the evidence suggests that these animals were uncommon visitors to southern Arizona, or perhaps missing altogether, after the end of the last ice age. Because Sonoita Valley grasslands survived and evolved without the presence of native hooved grazers for 10,000 years or more, they were unprepared for the introductions of domestic grazers that began with the Spanish in the sixteenth century. Compared to the Great Plains, grasslands of the Southwest have proved relatively fragile and intolerant of livestock activities. They also are less understood, because so many of them were altered almost out of existence by Europeans naïve about their nature and capacities. Their history was lost before anyone obtained a written or photographic record.

Beginning in the sixteenth century, and extending through most of the twentieth, threats to the integrity of Sonoita Valley grasslands came mostly in the form of domestic grazers. Most people lived off the land by grazing it with their cattle and horses. Today many more people are moving here just for the view, as ranchettes have replaced ranches and exurbanites have added their considerable numbers to the local human population. The future of the Sonoita Valley depends largely on the outcome of this latest human colonization.

Ranching and enjoying the view are honest and honorable things to do, as long as they are done with appropriate levels of care and concern for the future of the land. We have found that most ranchers in the valley have an abundance of both, as do most newcomers. But suppose the whole of the valley were nothing but one large cattle ranch, or one large housing development. What would be the consequences for regional biological diversity? Those species of plants and animals that thrive in the presence of cattle and houses would flourish, but those species that are intolerant of livestock grazing, or that require the wide-open spaces, would have relatively few places left to live. A diversity of landscapes, like a diversity of people, makes the world a richer, more interesting, and more sustainable place.

To protect a grassland we must first understand how it works. What are the key forces that shape the natural rhythms of birth and death, the flow of energy, and the cycling of nutrients? What roles do the various plants and animals play? Most important, how many people can live in the Sonoita Valley without compromising the very features that brought us here in the first place?

At what point along the continuum between wilderness and metropolis will the life-sustaining ecosystems of the valley begin to shut down and the richness of life be jeopardized? Can we develop reasonable guidelines that will meet the needs of all the living things in the valley, including humans? Facing this challenge involves two critical steps. First, we must learn all we can about the natural dynamics of the ecosystems in the valley, so that we can predict which of our activities the native flora and fauna will tolerate and which they will not. Then we must have the courage and the wisdom to live within those bounds. The first part involves good science. The second part involves good stewardship, and it will be much harder.

Attempting to understand the responses of the flora and fauna of the Sonoita Valley to changing environmental conditions has been at once exhilarating and humbling. Consider just four pairs of species. For every pygmy mouse that needs heavy grass cover, long protected from livestock, there is a silky pocket mouse that prefers the more heavily grazed pastures. For every prairie falcon that hunts best on the open uninterrupted prairie, there is a scaled quail whose daily water requirements are met ideally in

Bald Hill from the southeast

a place where everybody has a horse trough. For every plains lovegrass plant that lives in tight swards, there is a purple three-awn grass that colonizes only the heavily grazed substrates. For every cotton rat that likes the dense stands of sacaton grass, there is a deer mouse that prefers the more domesticated comforts of a garage or horse barn.

How do we provide opportunities for all this diversity, and what will be the ecological consequences if we do not? What will happen if we begin to subtract species of plants and animals one by one from the grasslands? The mosaic of life in the Sonoita Valley is intricate and complex, and its needs are many and varied. Yet most people agree that it deserves to be protected and sustained. The richness of life is what makes our own living here so interesting and sustaining. And, ultimately, we are as dependent upon the ecological services provided by these species as they are dependent upon our good will and stewardship for their very survival.

A principle as old as the scientific method is that for every experiment there must be a control. Otherwise there is no sure way of knowing the results of the experiment. The same principle applies to understanding the consequences of how we use the land. Without an unmanipulated landscape for comparison, how can we know whether a particular livestock grazing pattern, or irrigation scheme, or controlled burn, or zoning change, or increase in the density of homes or roads makes the grass grow better or worse? The climatic variability in the arid American West means that it rained either substantially more or substantially less in the years following the experiment than it did in

the years before, thus confounding the scientists' ability to distinguish the effects of the human experiment from those of the weather.

The only way to understand the impact of human activities in the Sonoita Valley would be to start with a large control area exempted insofar as possible from those activities and then to observe its behavior over a long period of time. In 1968, Ariel and Frank Appleton took all the livestock off their 8,000-acre Elgin Hereford Ranch at the eastern edge of the Sonoita Valley and created a control area they called the Research Ranch. It was an odd choice for a name, given that their idea was to find out what would happen when a place stopped *being* a ranch and to let nature run its course without human interference. But it was a brilliant idea—not only to protect a landscape from the human hand as much as possible, but also to measure what would happen to the place and to its plant and animal populations over time.

In 1980, thanks to the generosity of the Appleton family in giving their land, and to the Whittell Foundation for providing an operating endowment, the Research Ranch became part of the sanctuary system of the National Audubon Society. The purposes of the land remain the same as those conceived by Ariel and Frank in 1968. First, it is to serve as a refuge for all native plants and animals, especially those that do relatively poorly in areas used by people. Second, it is to be a control site, against which the ecological consequences of various land uses can be compared and therefore better understood.

The Research Ranch is an ideal control area because it is typical of the Sonoita Valley as a whole—a mixture of grass and oak and mesquite like that of nearly every ranch and housing development in the valley. This makes it different from most Audubon sanctuaries, which were established to protect places with exceptional or unusual biological diversity. Ecologically, the Research Ranch is a relatively ordinary piece of land, except that it is being treated in an extraordinary way.

In the early 1970s we began a series of projects whose collective goal was to learn some things about the natural history of the Research Ranch and of the Sonoita Valley as a whole, about the kinds of plants and animals that lived there, and about the impacts of environmental forces such as drought, fire, livestock grazing, and the spread of non-native vegetation. Subsequently we began to study how wild things in the valley respond to increasing numbers of people and to the houses, horses, dogs, roads, wells, and fences that accompany human migrations into modern exurban America. Our goal in this book is to place what we have learned into the broader context of the ecology, biological diversity, human history, and aesthetics of the Arizona borderlands.

What did the Sonoita Valley look like 400 or 4,000 years ago? Absent the gift of time travel, we can never know with certainty. Perhaps the best we can do is ask this question: What would happen to a little piece (say, about 8,000 acres) of the Sonoita Valley if we left it alone for a very long time? Might that little piece of land, the Research Ranch, eventually come to resemble what it was like in 1492? Does the ecological clock ever run backwards? Doubtless most managers, planners, and global-change entrepreneurs would scoff at such a notion. "You cannot turn back the clock," they would say. "Let us do more active

things than sit and watch the grass grow, and we will make it better." Here are some activities for "betterment" that have been used in the Sonoita Valley:

grazing to stimulate grass production;
dam building to hold back the flash-flood water;
ripping furrows in the grassland to increase water retention;
firefighting;
spraying with pesticides to control insects and weeds.

The skeptics would go on to say that the very idea of wilderness is nothing more than a mental construct. There are no landscapes that exist free of the human touch—not the Research Ranch of today, not even the Sonoita Valley of 400 or 4,000 years ago. Humans used it then, just as they do now. But you can bet that the same people who raise an eyebrow about wilderness would sell their souls to journey through time with us, to see what the Sonoita Valley looked like before there were cattle or railroads or fences or sport utility vehicles or homeowners' associations. We would like to tease them with the possibility that the Research Ranch can give us such a glimpse back: doubtless a blurred and distorted glimpse but perhaps a priceless peek nevertheless.

We have assembled the chapters and photographs that follow into three groups. First, we consider the major ecosystems of the Sonoita Valley. Next is a selection of stories about the diversity of living things in this part of the world. Some of the stories are based on studies on and adjacent to the Research Ranch, with an emphasis on the effects of fire, grazing, and exotic grasses. Others more broadly illustrate the variety of ways that plants and animals in the valley have evolved to deal with the physical environment and with one another. Finally, we add humans to the picture. How have people lived in the valley, and what have been the environmental consequences? What might things be like in the future?

As to the Research Ranch itself, one thing is certain: its most interesting stories cannot yet be told, because the place is still an ecological infant. In another hundred years, will the ranch be no more than an island in a suburban sea, or will the diversity and grandeur of the whole Sonoita Valley persist?

SONOITA PLAIN

Mustang Mountains from the entrance to the Research Ranch

THE SONOITA VALLEY is part of the basin-and-range country of southeastern Arizona—a rolling grassland sometimes interspersed with scattered trees, transected by stream channels that mostly are dry, and surrounded by wooded slopes leading up into adjacent hills and mountains. Horizons around the valley include the Santa Rita range to the west, the Huachuca Mountains in the east, and the Mustang and Whetstone Mountains to the north. The Canelo Hills frame the southern view. Riparian vegetation and wetlands follow two watercourses out of the valley. Sonoita Creek, a tributary of the Santa Cruz River, flows west and south. The Babocomari River flows east, into the San Pedro River. Two unincorporated towns in the valley are Sonoita in the west and Elgin in the east.

The Research Ranch is a bit south and east of Elgin. Three drainages cross the property, each flowing north into the Babocomari River, known by locals as Babocomari Creek. Vaughn Canyon and Lyle Canyon cross the sanctuary at its northwest and southeast corners, respectively, while most of the land is part of the O'Donnell Creek drainage. Two tributaries to O'Donnell Creek meet centrally on the ranch: Post Canyon from the southwest and Turkey Creek from the south.

Ecosystems of the Research Ranch are representative of the Sonoita Valley as a whole. Rolling open grasslands dominate the northern half of the sanctuary, while the plains become increasingly interspersed with oak and juniper as the land rises toward the Canelo Hills to the south. Scattered riparian trees and shrubs follow the drainages. Stream channels crossing the Research Ranch have flowing water only during the wettest periods, but three impoundments hold water most of the year: Finley Tank, Telles Tank, and Post Canyon Dam.

In the first part of this book, we consider those major environmental forces that determine the distribution and nature of the grassland, savanna, and wetland ecosystems that characterize the Sonoita Valley in general, and the Research Ranch in particular.

Periodic drought, frequent fire, and herbivorous (plant-eating) animals shape the geography and ecology of most of the world's grasslands, including those of the Southwest. Because each of these forces is inherently episodic, grasslands can be unstable places. Droughts come and go under the influence of global climatic events. Grasslands burn when enough dry fuel has accumulated to carry fire from one plant to the next. Trees are less likely to survive a fire than are grasses. Herbivorous animals wax and wane as their resources dictate. Although southwestern grasslands apparently lacked the nomadic herds of large grazing mammals characteristic of most of the world's great grasslands, they did not lack for herbivory itself, as any Sonoita Valley resident can testify who has dealt with periodic and dramatic outbreaks of grasshoppers. And since the introduction of livestock, hooved grazers have been as important here as in East Africa or across the North American Great Plains.

Given the importance of precipitation, fire, and herbivory, it is appropriate that the first three chapters of this section give consideration to their particular effects. Next in importance are interactions among the species themselves, involved as they are in ecological and evolutionary contests for limited resources, including each other. This is the topic of chapter four.

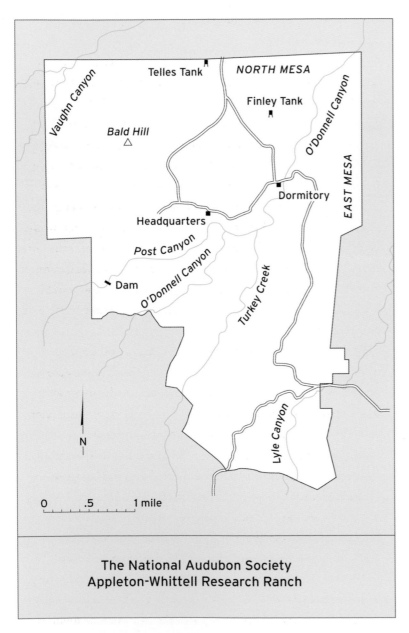

Vaughn Canyon

Telles Tank

NORTH MESA

Finley Tank

O'Donnell Canyon

Bald Hill
△

EAST MESA

Dormitory

Headquarters

Post Canyon

O'Donnell Canyon

Dam

Turkey Creek

Lyle Canyon

N

0   .5   1 mile

**The National Audubon Society
Appleton-Whittell Research Ranch**

In chapter five we discuss the grassland trees—the oak, mesquite, and juniper that almost certainly have reached higher densities and spread farther onto the Research Ranch and across the Sonoita Valley than they did two centuries ago. These are the trees that combine with the grasses to make a savanna. There may be no ecosystem more important in human evolutionary history than a savanna.

Another critical environmental variable in the Sonoita Valley is the amount of water at the surface and in the ground (chapter six). It is water that grows the great riparian woodlands, that supplies pools and streams, and that sustains an extraordinary amount of biological diversity. No ecosystems have suffered more grievously in the Southwest than those dependent on standing or flowing water. The Sonoita Valley is no exception to this pattern. Nevertheless, some open waters and riparian woodlands remain, and they are among the valley's most treasured and important places.

Finally, above all of the Sonoita Valley spreads the magnificent southwestern sky (chapter seven).

PEOPLE OF THE NORTH have asked us many times why we would want to spend summers in Arizona, not just winters.

"Isn't it awfully *hot* down there in the desert?" they ask.

"Well, sure, sometimes it is hot," we reply. "But the *real* problems are the humidity and the mosquitoes and the chiggers, and getting your car stuck in a flooded wash."

Most people think of the Southwest as a hot and a dry place. However, at nearly 5,000 feet in elevation, the Sonoita Valley is as likely to have winter snow as it is to reach 100 degrees Fahrenheit in the summer. Average annual precipitation is between sixteen and seventeen inches. The valley can become very cold in winter. This is far from the climate of a true desert.

Like the entire Southwest, the valley has two rainy seasons. Fairly predictable summer monsoon rains fall from July to early September, and less predictable winter rains fall mainly between November and March. Fronts bringing winter precipitation come from the Pacific; often they are the tail ends of storms that already have dropped most of their moisture in California. Because of the cold, few native grasses and wildflowers respond to winter precipitation, though good winter rains can help the trees and shrubs and the water table in the Sonoita Valley over the long term.

May and June are the hottest and driest months in southeastern Arizona. This is a difficult time. Everybody in the West knows what it is like to wait for the end of a drought, but usually for them it is not an annual ordeal. Around Sonoita a drought happens almost every year, for about two months beginning in May. Just when everything in New York or Indiana or Colorado is about to celebrate spring, all the living things in southern Arizona—the plants, the animals, and the people—shut down and wait.

The fact that the drought breaks almost every July doesn't make the waiting any easier. Each day we search the sky, consult with our neighbors, and look for clouds. The further it gets into July without rain, the greater the daily angst. Was that moisture we smelled in the air at dawn? Did that incessant west wind fade a bit and give way to a breeze from the south or east? We know that elusive Mexican blessing, the summer monsoon, is down there in Chihuahua or Sonora or somewhere. It is building the annual momentum that will drive moisture our way—up off the Gulf of Mexico and Gulf of California and into the air over our mountains. Then the sun (we always have plenty of that) can put energy into the moist air, and lift it so it can cool, and build in it those great thunderclouds that will roll out over the valley and bring us life.

Old-timers tell us that the monsoon comes on the Fourth of July. What they really mean is that July Fourth is the date when everybody officially starts to worry about the monsoon, which frequently comes a little later than that. How much later depends on the year, and that is part of the problem.

Commencing in late June, clouds stop being wispy and turn puffy, as gulf air replaces Pacific air. June lightning brings some wildfires. This is the natural season for fire in the valley, but it is not yet the season for rain. There can be a June sprinkle, just a tease, but that doesn't count. The grasses are not fooled, because they have evolved to know that the real rain comes in July.

That first summer rain falls in the form of plops, not drops. It is an extremely sensual happening, and locals go a little crazy. Otherwise rational adults, along with the kids, march about as

Snow on agave

Standing water after the first monsoon rain, O'Donnell Canyon

Standing water and algae in a catchment basin near Ranch Headquarters

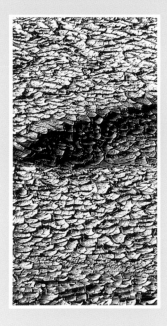

Drying mud, O'Donnell Canyon

the rain falls on their heads and the puddles wet their toes. The first serious rain plops mix with the dust, and there is a smell that one does not forget. We all become instant rain scientists, with plastic and only moderately accurate rain gauges placed near but not next to our homes. A gauge tucked in too close to the house might miss a whole downpour being driven sideways before the wind. That would be tragic, because measuring and comparing precipitation amounts to the nearest hundredth of an inch is the main form of social interchange in the Sonoita Valley, especially in July and August. Anything less than 1/100th of an inch in the rain gauge is officially a "trace." Perhaps it is a good thing that most people in the Sonoita Valley have not yet adopted the metric system. Dividing traces into fractions of millimeters and then squabbling over whose trace was the biggest would take up even more time.

Because of broad vistas across the valley, it usually is pretty clear who got a *good* rain on any particular day and who did not. Summer thundershowers can be remarkably local, so the washes may be running full in one place while the dust has scarcely settled only a few hundred yards away. Because a half-dozen heavy showers can make up the bulk of the total summer's rainfall, and because summer rain is what makes the grass grow, it is perfectly possible that some little place in the Sonoita Valley might scarcely turn green at all in any particular year. If that little place happens to be your backyard, you feel victimized. It is easy to become jealous of the neighbor whose problem is a leaky roof.

Because of the patchy and uncertain behavior of the monsoon, it is important not to make assumptions about personal matters such as how much rain your neighbor actually received. Never boast when you were one of "those folks over there that got rain yesterday." Never, ever, call up your neighbor and say something like, "Wasn't that just the most incredible rain we had last night?" Instead, you ask politely and with seeming casualness, "Did you get some rain yesterday?" If they did not, you say something like, "Oh, I am so sorry." If they did, they may ask you for your hundredths, and then you may tell them. But never volunteer.

Once the monsoon has come, if it has been a good one, the grasslands of the Sonoita Valley turn from burnt umber to green, and the rolling hills of Wales come to mind. Not all years are verdant, however. Historical and paleontological evidence verifies that prolonged dry periods are inevitable in this part of the world. Only a foolish rancher does not have a plan for dealing with a drought that lasts longer than the usual premonsoon months of May and June. Since nearly all human residents of the valley depend on wells for domestic water, a major long-term concern is whether the rains can recharge the groundwater at the same rate it is being depleted.

Human population density in the Sonoita Valley likely will be limited by water. As for the native plants and animals, drought is a part of their common evolutionary heritage. Each is prepared to hunker down in a dry year and wait it out. Most individuals do not survive, but enough do to repopulate the region once the rains return. This sort of population dynamic is common in the natural world, but it is largely foreign to modern humans. No one knows what will happen if the wells start to give out.

TWO · Fire

ON APRIL 29, 2002, a wildfire of human origin ignited near the Mexican border south of the Sonoita Valley. Driven by fierce winds, the so-called Ryan Fire eventually consumed nearly 40,000 acres, including more than 80 percent of the Research Ranch. The Ryan Fire was contained three days later in the grasslands of Fort Huachuca. Thanks to heroic efforts by Linda Kennedy and others on the Audubon staff, all sanctuary structures were saved except two old barns. Unfortunately, the Appleton home on the property was completely lost. Just after the fire, a Tucson television crew interviewed Ariel Appleton's eldest son, Bryce, as they stood before the charred remains of his mother's house.

"This place is not about the buildings," Bryce said. "It is about the land." Clearly, that was not the sorrowful sound bite our local crash-and-bash news team had been looking for. Bryce Appleton had it right, of course, but you had to admire his presence of mind under the circumstances.

But what *about* the land and its living things? How have the grasslands, oak woodlands, mesquite savannas, and riparian floodplains on the Research Ranch responded to the Ryan Fire? As we write this, it is too early to make a final judgment. There is good reason for optimism and some reason for concern.

The conditions necessary and sufficient for fire in natural ecosystems include a source of ignition (such as lightning or anthropogenic burning), warm temperature, and an adequate quantity of dry fuel. These conditions frequently are met in the grasslands and savannas of the American Southwest, and the ecological importance of fire in the region has long been recognized. However, over the past century the natural sizes, frequencies,

and intensities of fires have been reduced by disturbances such as livestock grazing, landscape fragmentation, and fire suppression efforts. As a result researchers have only a limited understanding of the role fire may once have played in sustaining biodiversity and shaping the structure and function of ecosystems in the Arizona borderlands. We suspect, and limited evidence suggests, that in the days before fires became scarce, open grasslands were more common, while woodlands and shrublands were more restricted. This is because although most grasses are relatively tolerant of fire, many woody plants are not.

Immediately following the Ryan Fire a local rancher support group called the Cowbelles put up signs along the highway near Sonoita that said "Grazing Prevents Blazing." It seemed like odd timing, because the fire had started on a cattle ranch, most of the land that burned was being grazed, and some livestock were killed. Nevertheless, the Cowbelles had a point.

After livestock were removed from the Research Ranch, fuels that once fed the cattle remained on the ground and began to feed fires. The first two notable burns we studied happened in 1974. A hunter probably started one of them. The other began when somebody with limited field experience tidied up his barbecue by tossing the used (but still warm) charcoal briquettes over the back fence. Other fires followed over the years, some set deliberately as part of field experiments, others set by lightning or by accident. From them all, a generally consistent pattern emerged, providing insight into the effects of fire on vegetation and wildlife in the absence of livestock in this part of the world.

Soil is an excellent insulator. Grass plants usually survive fire because they grow from their root crowns at or below the soil

9

Hillside west of Turkey Creek after the April 2002 Ryan Fire

Fire-scarred agave

Burned agave

Postfire landscape, two and a half months after the Ryan Fire of April 2002

Same landscape, three and a half months after the Ryan Fire of April 2002

surface, not from the tips of their branches like trees or shrubs. We found that it takes two or at most three postfire growing seasons for most grasses at the Research Ranch to fully return to preburn condition. Meanwhile, the soil surface is opened up for an abundance of wildflowers to sprout from their previously grass-covered soil seed banks. Since the flora of the Research Ranch includes many more kinds of wildflowers than grass species, fire plays a critical role in sustaining plant biodiversity.

Woody plants in the Sonoita Valley respond individually to fire, depending on their ability to resprout from roots or stems after burning. Mesquite trees are good at this sort of recovery, as range managers and ranchers have learned in their often-futile efforts to use fire to control the spread of mesquite into formerly open grasslands. Repeated burning might eventually kill mesquite, especially if the fires are hot enough, but even on the Research Ranch most of these trees have survived. By contrast, oaks and especially the riparian trees such as cottonwood and sycamore are more likely to suffer long-term damage or even death from fire.

Few grassland animals are killed outright by fire. We have found some dead rattlesnakes and lizards on recently burned ground, probably because they were too slow to reach safety ahead of the wind-driven flames. For example, the Ryan Fire took less than an hour to pass from one side of the Research Ranch's 8,000 acres to the other. Rodents can get into their burrows in time, while birds and large mammals fly or run away. Nevertheless, fires at the Research Ranch have had dramatic short-term effects on birds and mammals because of resulting changes in cover and food.

The first two winters after a fire are a great bonus for migra-tory birds. They come in pursuit of wildflower seeds that have been produced in conspicuous abundance because of the relatively open ground. Mourning doves, vesper sparrows, horned larks, lark sparrows, and savannah sparrows are common in winter on the Research Ranch in areas that have recently burned. By contrast, many ground-nesting summer birds require the thatch of old grass to conceal their eggs and young from predators. As a result, birds such as Montezuma quail and Cassin's, Botteri's, and grasshopper sparrows will avoid a burn until a sufficient number of postfire monsoon seasons have built the grass cover back to its preburn condition. Fire does an equally impressive job of rearranging grassland rodents in the Sonoita Valley, generally favoring pocket mice and kangaroo rats (which hunt seeds and avoid predators better on relatively open ground), while temporarily discouraging species such as cotton rats and pygmy mice (which feed on the grass foliage and need to hide from predators under heavy cover).

The lesson learned from earlier burns at the Research Ranch is that a heterogeneity of landscapes in various stages of postfire change will provide ecological opportunities for the greatest variety of living things. We came to this conclusion by studying the responses of plants and animals to fire across time and, critically, by comparing our field data with those taken from large portions of the Research Ranch that had not burned at least since the sanctuary was established in 1968.

We had five reasons to suspect that consequences of the Ryan Fire might be different from those of earlier burns we have studied in the Sonoita Valley. First, there was greater-than-average plant biomass heading into the fall of 2001. This was especially true for a number of wildflowers known to contain quantities of highly volatile chemicals in their stems and foliage. Second, the winter and spring of 2001–2002 had seen one of the most severe droughts in a century of Arizona weather records, so all that volatile fuel was tinder-dry. Third, the winds on April 29 and 30, 2002, were exceptionally strong. Fourth, the early date of the fire (compared to the natural lightning season later in June) left the land in an exposed and parched condition for an unusually long period—until the monsoon began in mid-July. Finally, the size of the Ryan Fire created a very large blackened landscape that presented challenges to recolonization for any species driven off by the burn.

All of these factors—fuels, drought, wind, timing, and size—meant that the Ryan Fire stressed plant and animal populations on the Research Ranch to a degree we had not seen before. How much grass mortality was there? How many trees were killed? How soon would the grass-dependent animals come back?

Like every new event on the Research Ranch, the Ryan Fire presented an opportunity to watch and to learn and to expand our understanding. But it was hard to be objective, especially at first. The ground was black all through May and June of 2002. In the uplands, only the yerba-de-pasmo shrubs looked to be thriving. In the bottomlands, some of the tall sacaton grass began to sprout, but many of the clumps looked dead. Most of the oaks had dropped their leaves because of the drought, and they bore fresh fire scars as well; we would not know until after the monsoon rains how many had survived the fire. The agaves and the yuccas were scorched, as were some of the biggest sycamores and cottonwoods on the sanctuary, and we could not tell how many of them would make it.

The monsoon was a little late in 2002, but by the end of July there had been some good rains, and the Sonoita Valley began to turn green. Soon a carpet of young plants replaced the blackened ash fields of the Research Ranch, and our spirits rose. Some of the oaks made new leaves, though many did not. Grass mortality was high in places, especially on rocky slopes with little soil where the combination of drought stress and fire looked to have been fatal. Wildflowers were having a banner year almost everywhere, and they dominated the green carpet to a degree we had seen only rarely. Botteri's and Cassin's sparrows were gone, and most were likely to stay away for at least one more summer. But the place was alive with lark sparrows and horned larks, and we had live-trapped numerous silky pocket mice and hispid pocket mice in our rodent survey work.

By late in the monsoon season of 2003, more Botteri's and Cassin's sparrows were around than in the first summer after the fire, but in many places the grass remained sparse. Whole hillsides looked green enough, but most of the vegetation still consisted of wildflowers. We were becoming convinced that the Ryan Fire had damaged some grasslands on the Research Ranch to a degree we had not seen before. In many places grass cover was significantly higher on adjacent cattle ranches than it was on the sanctuary. Almost certainly this was because the lower fuels reduced the fire's intensity in grazed areas, so that more of the grass survived. The Cowbelles were looking more insightful by the day.

We have revised our model about the effects of fire on southwestern grasslands to include what we learned from the Ryan burn. When a drought comes and the wind blows, and fuels have accumulated over decades without grazing or burning, then fire can be more destructive to plant life than we previously thought possible. Perhaps low-intensity fires were more common in the past, forestalling catastrophic grassland fires by keeping down the fuels.

The return to preburn conditions will take a large and uncertain number of years on the Research Ranch because of the Ryan Fire. Perhaps some of the grassland patterns we describe in the next chapter will turn out to have been permanently altered. Which grasses will return where, and when, and in what order? With luck we will be there to see it happen.

THE WHITE LIGHT of a noontime sun flattens nearly all contour out of the rolling plain that dominates the Sonoita Valley. Only the surrounding mountains add relief, and even these can get lost in a bluish haze, especially during the desert days of May and June. But the locals know every tooth and notch of the jagged skyline that surrounds their valley, and they take comfort in its familiarity when other features are obscured by season and time of day.

The topography of the valley best emerges when the sun is at either horizon, and especially when the monsoon brings life to the grasses. The highest places are level mesas and rolling upland knolls. Cattle prefer to graze in these areas, probably because of the ease of walking. Slopes lead progressively down from the mesas through a series of benches, or terraces. Alternating periods of downcutting and deposition during and since the Pleistocene created these terraces and their intervening slopes. Finally, at the bottom of the gradient there are the current floodplains, where water sometimes flows when the monsoon comes. Cattle like the bottomlands, especially in early summer before the uplands turn green.

More than eighty different species of grasses can be found in the Sonoita Valley. Before we undertake to describe where the most important of them live, we need to say something about their names. Scientists use officially sanctioned Latin binomials (usually written in *italics)* to identify species, and these are invaluable for their precision, universality, and relative permanence. But the scientific names of grasses are exotic and sterile words compared to the common names given to them by ranchers. Because the goals of this book are to convey the aesthetics and the ecology

of the Sonoita Valley, we have included both the common and the scientific names of the species mentioned in this book at the end, in an appendix. In the text we will stick with the common names, which almost invariably have a friendlier ring to them.

Over a century ago the naturalist C. Hart Merriam recognized and described elevational belts of vegetation he called life zones, extending from low desert to alpine tundra in northern Arizona. Life zones are present in the Sonoita Valley, too, albeit expressed across yards instead of miles and across a topographic gradient from floodplain to adjacent low terrace, and from there up the slopes to the mesas and rolling hilltops. How do the grasses change along this topographic gradient—across these Sonoita Valley life zones—and how are the patterns affected by such things as fire and livestock grazing?

Broader floodplains in the Sonoita Valley are dominated by giant sacaton, a true tallgrass of the Southwest that reaches more than seven feet in height when conditions are right. Sacaton thrives where the soils are deep and frequently watered by the gentle meanderings of braided streams. Historically, this grass has found itself in harm's way. Heavy grazing in the late 1800s diminished the capacity of watersheds to hold precipitation and release it gradually throughout the year. Formerly perennial streams became seasonal, and flash floods carved stream channels deeper, scouring away some sacaton while starving adjacent stands for water.

Terraces adjacent to sacaton bottomlands also have deep soils, but they receive less water. On these terraces, blue grama is likely to be most abundant, often mixed with sparser populations

Overview of Research Ranch topography from East Mesa

Snow-covered hills with agaves, near Turkey Creek

*Left to right: Curly-mesquite, Cane beardgrass,
Blue grama, Plains lovegrass*

of vine-mesquite, sideoats grama, and a variety of other grasses. Blue grama is one of the most widespread grasses in all of North America. It is dominant across much of the western Great Plains, and it is distributed from the Valley of Mexico to the Prairie Provinces of Canada. Blue grama is nutritious and also highly tolerant of grazing, as befits any grass whose evolutionary history includes an association with bison. Blue grama is the most abundant native grass today in the Sonoita Valley, but that probably is a historical artifact of livestock grazing, because bison rarely strayed into this part of the world after the close of the last ice age.

The highest points on the Research Ranch, the mesas and rolling hilltops, support the greatest variety of grasses, and no one species is likely to dominate. Blue grama grows there, but it is more evenly mixed with close relatives such as hairy grama and sprucetop grama and with more distantly related species such as plains lovegrass, wolftail, curly-mesquite, a variety of three-awn grasses, and a curious bluestem relative called cane beardgrass that never dominates but always sticks up above the rest.

Among this suite of upland grasses, those of shorter stature—especially the gramas and curly-mesquite—generally are the ones that grow best in the presence of livestock, for at least two reasons. First, any grass that grows better horizontally than vertically is putting less of its tissue up where the cattle can get at it. Second, a tall grass will outcompete a short grass for light as long as it can get enough water. If "the enemy of my enemy is my

friend," then a cow turns out to be a friend of the little sprucetop grama plant struggling to get out from under the canopy of a taller plains lovegrass.

For grasses that grow on the steeper hillsides in the Sonoita Valley, everything depends upon soil and compass direction. North-facing slopes are cooler and therefore effectively wetter than south-facing slopes. Oaks grow there for this reason, and they further increase shading for the grasses. Texas bluestem is a relatively tall species that is nearly restricted on the Research Ranch to north-facing slopes under oaks.

Soils on slopes are drier than those on level uplands or bottomlands because water tends to run off them rather than to soak into the ground. The resulting erosion slows the rate of soil development on slopes, and the shallower soils can retain less water for plants because of their lesser mass per unit of land area. Rocky south-facing slopes represent an especially extreme physical environment because of their exposure to the drying power of the sun. Nevertheless, a variety of grasses can be abundant on such places in the Sonoita Valley, including some midheight forms such as sideoats grama and tanglehead. One reason that relatively tall grasses often grow on slopes is that livestock prefer to graze on level mesas and bottomlands, where the walking is easier.

What did the grasslands of the Sonoita Valley look like before the arrival of European peoples and their livestock? We have some clues based on the abundance and distribution of the grasses since livestock were removed from the Research Ranch in 1968. The taller bunchgrasses have increased on the sanctuary, and they almost certainly were more widespread and abundant in the Sonoita Valley in 1492 than they are today. But how much more abundant were they, and which species dominated? What were the effects, back then, of fire and of drought?

Thousands of cattle and horses grazed on the Sonoita Plain in the early 1890s, brought there by Europeans who had little idea about the long-term carrying capacity of the land and no idea at all that this was a grassland that had evolved without bison. Then a series of years came that were virtually without summer rain, and the whole system collapsed. The great drought and grazing events of the 1890s not only destroyed most of the grass but probably also resulted in the loss of topsoil. Those soils have not come close to recovering, and they probably will not do so on a time scale relevant to the humans now living in the valley.

How might the topography of grasses have changed after the 1890s? Consider the case of cane beardgrass, the tallest species that dots uplands across the Sonoita Valley but that never seems to become numerically dominant. Actually, it frequently *is* the most common grass in one place—along the edges of roads. Why might that be? Roadsides usually are not grazed, but if that were the only factor that mattered, then cane beardgrass should be a dominant grass on many parts of the Research Ranch, and it is not. Roads, however, are places where the soil has been graded and raised and, if the grading is properly done, where water runs off when it rains. In other words, the edges of the roads probably have more soil, and they almost certainly get more water. Might not roadsides more nearly represent conditions as they were across the Sonoita Valley as a whole in 1492, when the soils were deeper and the rain was more likely to soak in than to run off? Might not cane beardgrass once have been a dominant grass? We likely will never know, but the urge to speculate is irresistible. Who would turn down the opportunity to visit the prehistoric Sonoita Valley and count the cane beardgrass if such a thing were possible?

FOUR ~ Eat and Be Eaten

SOMETIMES IN THE SONOITA VALLEY, grasshoppers seem to outnumber the blades of grass. Ranchers dislike these voracious insects because of the massive amounts of forage they consume that might otherwise be available to livestock. Those of us with the temerity to have a garden know how they can move in and chow down. Some people object to the crunching sound their exoskeletons make when they are driven over on the highway. Sometimes, in late August or early September, the roads in the valley become almost slippery with the bodies of smashed grasshoppers. Yet despite their abundance, grasshoppers rarely consume everything in sight. What stops them before that happens? One clue comes from the behavior of the grasshoppers. When we have taken the trouble to watch grasshoppers at the Research Ranch, we have noticed that they actually spend relatively little time eating, and most of their time apparently watching us back. In other words, grasshoppers are wary animals, and in that behavior we have a clue about the whole system of which they are a part.

Grasshoppers are herbivores (plant-eaters), and they provide a superb illustration of how the balance of biological communities can be established—by the upward flow of energy through a food chain and potential control of that same food chain from the top down—by predators. A grasshopper population in such a system might be limited in two distinctly different ways: the first is by food, and the other is by being food. Grasshoppers with a particular fondness for plains lovegrass might well be limited by the availability of their preferred forage. But they might also be limited by the predatory actions of any of a variety of small birds with a fondness for insects, such as the horned lark, cactus wren, or Cassin's sparrow.

Are populations of herbivorous grasshoppers controlled from the bottom of the food chain upward, by the amount of plant food made available to them? Or are they limited from the top of the food chain down, by predators such as the horned lark? For that matter, what limits the number of horned larks? Is it the abundance of grasshoppers, or could it be another predator up the line, such as the prairie falcon? Ecologists have spent much time attempting to learn which possibility—bottom-up versus top-down control, is the more likely.

At first glance it seems logical that control would come from the bottom up. After all, only green plants can use the energy of the sun to build more of themselves from nutrients they find in the soil, air, and water. Plant abundance, then, determines the numbers of herbivores, and these populations in turn regulate the numbers of predators that feed on the plant-eaters. Layered-in at each level are the parasites that live in or on the bodies of plants, herbivores, and predators. It is no surprise that there are more kinds of parasites in the world than any other sort of organism, given the variety of their ecological opportunities.

Ecologists are certain about the preceding scenario as to the bottom-up flow of energy and nutrients, that is, the resource dependence of one link in a food chain on the adjacent one that is closer to the sun. The issue of food-chain *control* is another matter. Field observations and the results of field experiments suggest that ecosystem control is equally likely to come from the top down.

Take the plains-lovegrass-to-horned-lark-to-prairie-falcon food chain as a hypothetical illustration. It certainly is possible that the growth of plains lovegrass determines the number of grasshoppers, which limits the number of horned larks, which in

2 5

Panther grasshopper

turn affects the number of prairie falcons. But another possibility exists. Suppose the prairie falcons are such skilled and efficient aerial hunters that they limit the horned larks to a number below the level where they can control the number of grasshoppers. This situation permits the grasshoppers to reach very high numbers, which in turn makes it likely that grasshopper herbivory, rather than sunlight or nutrients, limits the abundance of plains lovegrass. This is top-down control. Its most important feature is that the abundance and skill of the top predator is what determines the nature of the whole ecosystem. As just described, prairie falcons are allies of grasshoppers and enemies of plains lovegrass because of their impacts on horned larks. But suppose something happens to prairie falcons, and they disappear from

the Sonoita Valley. Now the horned larks are in control, the grasshoppers are in trouble, and the plains lovegrass never had it so good.

Most species except the very top carnivores probably have experienced both top-down and bottom-up control during their evolutionary histories. That is why nearly all species show clear evidence of knowing how to compete for limited resources, while simultaneously avoiding predation. No species has perfect competitive or antipredator abilities, because natural selection works equally strongly in favor of the competitors and the predators. Sooner or later, any species will be eliminated that cannot play at least to an overall tie in this evolutionary contest.

The environmental implications of top-down control are

Barberpole grasshopper

clear and serious. In ecosystems where this is the operating rule, elimination of a top predator can change the landscape far beyond the simple loss of one charismatic species. The Sonoita Valley of 200 years ago undoubtedly supported good populations of two major predators, the mountain lion and the Mexican wolf. Some of their most important prey were mule deer and white-tailed deer, and these in turn fed heavily on certain shrubs such as mountain mahogany and cliff rose. It is possible (even likely) that the shrubs thrived in the old days because wolves and mountain lions held down the numbers of deer. Now the wolves are gone, exterminated by Europeans who also persecuted the mountain lions. Why, then, are mountain mahogany and cliff rose still common in the valley? Perhaps the reason is that they never were controlled by deer (top down), but by their abilities to obtain water and other nutrients that are scarce in an arid land (bottom up). More likely, the shrubs persist because another deer predator has come along to replace the wolves and mountain lions—namely, us.

Humans are the world's most important predators and herbivores, controlling many ecosystems from the top down. The main reason humans persecute other predators is not because they might eat us. It is because they represent the competition. Ranchers in the old days killed wolves because they feared for the safety of their cattle, not their children. Once the other predators are gone, we may have little alternative but to act in their place, lest the herbivores overrun their food supplies and destabilize whole ecosystems. This has happened in many places across North America, where, for example, deer populations have exploded in the absence of human or other predators. This is the main ecological justification for hunting; but significant risks are associated with inserting ourselves as top predators into ecosystems whose complexities we scarcely understand.

A few years ago, in a combined mathematics and ecology course, we attempted to model long-term population relationships between wolves and deer. With the right numbers in the model, deer and wolves could coexist indefinitely. But with only small increases in the numbers of wolves, the deer would go quickly to extinction, followed by the wolves. The lesson here is that attempting to manage ecosystems by regulating populations is a risky and difficult business. The future of predators and prey in the Sonoita Valley are in human hands. But it probably will be wiser and simpler to leave them alone as much as possible, to sort things out for themselves as they did for millennia prior to our arrival.

WE REFER IN THIS BOOK to a place called the Sonoita Plain and to another place called the Sonoita Valley. Sometimes we use these terms interchangeably, but in fact the valley is bigger than the plain and encloses it. The difference has to do with trees, which a plain lacks by definition. The fringes of the Sonoita Valley and the adjacent foothills probably have been wooded for a very long time, but the boundaries between plains and woodlands are unstable tension zones, where grass and trees compete for supremacy. At those places where a grassland grades into a woodland, the trees have broad spreading crowns that do not touch and that leave room for the grasses below. Such places are called savannas. The best-known savannas are those of East Africa, but the American Southwest has its share.

A number of factors affect the spread of trees into grasslands and determine the nature and position of savannas. Perhaps the most important of these is fire, which tends to keep grasslands relatively free of woody plants (see chapter two). Grazing animals facilitate the growth of savannas, both by eating the grassy fuels that otherwise would carry fire from one tree to the next, and in some cases by dispersing tree seeds in their feces. Alternatively, animals that browse on woody vegetation might favor grasslands. Finally, seasonal distribution of rainfall can be very important. In the Southwest, nearly all grasses respond only to summer rain, whereas the trees can take advantage of rainfall in both winter and summer. Episodes of increased cool-season rainfall probably encouraged the spread of trees and shrubs into southwestern grasslands historically, and this will happen again if future climate change involves a shift away from dominance by the summer monsoonal thundershowers.

The most important savanna trees in the Sonoita Valley are juniper, mesquite, and oak. Both alligator and one-seed juniper grow here, usually mixed in with the more common oaks. Junipers may have been more abundant historically than they are today. People harvested many of these trees in the late nineteenth and early twentieth centuries for fenceposts and mine timbers, because of their decay-resistant wood. Today, the mines are closed, steel fenceposts are replacing their wooden predecessors, and junipers are making a comeback. They also may benefit from fire suppression. Dispersal of junipers into grasslands is facilitated by a thrush called the Townsend's solitaire, a bird that eats almost nothing in winter besides juniper berries.

⬦

Mesquite trees were reported to be largely confined to stream banks prior to the drought and overgrazing events of the late 1800s. Then the resultant openings in the grassland sod became colonization sites for mesquite seeds, and many of the formerly open plains became a new kind of savanna. Once the trees became established, they were difficult to remove. Their roots can reach many meters into the soil, greatly exceeding the heights of aboveground tree parts.

Cattle growers and range managers frequently describe mesquite trees as ranching nuisances, because they can rob the grasses of sunlight, water, and other nutrients. It is largely a self-inflicted wound, because the seeds of mesquite germinate best when they have passed through the gut of an herbivore such as a cow or a horse. The Spanish introduction of horses into the New World likely increased the mobility of mesquite as well as of Native Americans.

Overlooking O'Donnell Canyon toward the Mustangs, late fall

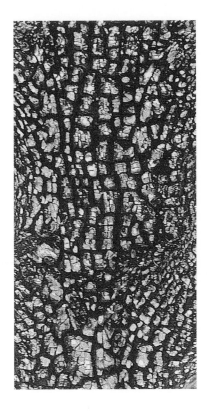

Burned trunk of Emory oak

Despite having a generally bad reputation, mesquite is a useful tree. The wood makes good fenceposts, as well as firewood for homes and restaurants (particularly for mesquite-grilled meats). Many of the larger trees have disappeared, because the logs from the huge old ones served as cross beams in territorial buildings and as polished shelves in homes and bookstores. Mesquite beans were a valuable food for Native Americans, especially during times of crop failure. Early ranchers fed the beans to their livestock when droughts diminished the grasses. Connoisseurs and other locals highly value mesquite honey to this day.

A wonderful array of songs, stories, and poems exists for oak trees throughout the northern hemisphere. Sonoita Valley oaks are not stately compared to their eastern and Old World counterparts, and the literati appear to have missed them, so far. Nevertheless, they are a beautiful and defining element of the valley. At a point along State Highway 83 in the drive from Tucson, the climb suddenly brings you up out of the desert and into the oaks. At that same point the first overview of the Sonoita Valley lies before you. What a sight!

Both Arizona white oak and the Emory oak are common on the southern half of the Research Ranch and elsewhere around the margins of the valley. Botanists classify them as a white oak and a black oak, respectively, but this distinction has little to do with their actual appearance. Like most things in nature, they are neither black nor white but subtly different shades of brown and gray. To our eyes, the bark of an Emory oak is browner, and the cracks in it form a checkered pattern. The bark of an Arizona white oak is relatively gray and more longitudinally furrowed than checked.

Sonoita Valley oaks are called evergreen because they don't shed their leaves in the winter. However, many of them do drop their leaves in the hot and dry times of May and June, especially in years and places where drought stress is high. When the rains show up in July, so do the new leaves. The oaks often flower just before the monsoon arrives, and the acorns grow to maturity by late summer or fall. Oak trees live a long time—easily a century or more in the Sonoita Valley. Given the size of a bumper acorn crop on even a single Emory oak, and the fact that each acorn holds the promise of becoming another tree, it is hard not to wonder why the valley isn't a solid oak forest. Of course, most of those acorns never sprout. Instead they rot on the ground or serve as food for birds, squirrels, collared peccaries, livestock, and, especially in times past, people.

Dispersal of oaks into grasslands is made possible by two animals that harvest and bury acorns for future use—the rock squirrel and the Mexican jay (see chapter ten). In years of good oak reproduction, the squirrels and jays will bury more acorns than they eventually harvest. It is these few forgotten individuals that represent the seeds of the next generation of oaks. Rock squirrels and Mexican jays are among the wildlife attracted to houses and gardens because of the extra water, food, and shelter (see chapter eighteen). This is another reason, besides fire suppression, why oaks eventually might win the battle with grasses for landscape supremacy in developing parts of the Sonoita Valley.

As conservationists with a passion for plains and prairies, we have been frustrated at times by well-intentioned citizens who speak as if a grassland were no more than some sort of badly managed and severely disturbed forest. As ecologists, we recognize that nearly all grasslands live in a state of dynamic tension with nearby woodlands and that the grassland trees clearly have their places. Both ecologically and aesthetically, a savanna may be the best thing of all.

In the 1970s a biologist from Kenya visited the Research Ranch. After touring the property he remarked to us that it reminded him of home, except there were no giraffes stretching their necks up into the savanna trees. Given our common African ancestry, perhaps savannas remind all humans of home in some deeper sense. Perhaps part of the lure of the Sonoita Valley is that it tugs at those evolutionary roots.

I N THE SUMMER OF 1851, a Colorado pikeminnow left the San Pedro River and swam upstream into the Sonoita Valley. It followed the Babocomari River and then moved south up O'Donnell Canyon into what is now the Research Ranch. The pikeminnow passed numerous beaver lodges along the way. The fish was over three feet long. Fanciful? Well, we aren't sure about the year, but we've got the right century, the right mammal, and the right big fish. No other facts make it more startlingly clear how much things have changed since the middle of the nineteenth century. Gone are the waters that once flowed in sufficient quantity and with sufficient regularity to invite such a magnificent fish into the valley. Gone too are the beaver that built their lodges at the water's edge.

What happened to all that water? One view holds that livestock grazing changed the watersheds of the Southwest. Both the summer monsoon and the winter rains once soaked into the soil and recharged subterranean aquifers that could sustain the perennial streams, even during periods of relative drought. Then livestock grazing removed so much of the grass that the rains began to wash away the soil rather than soaking into it. What followed were episodes of violent flash floods and erosion during wet periods and dry creek beds the rest of the time. An alternative explanation is that climatic change (including drought) was the culprit and that most of the flowing waters of the Sonoita Valley were doomed with or without cattle. We know that severe droughts occurred in the 1890s, 1930s, and 1950s. However, livestock grazing must have exacerbated the impacts of these droughts on the grass, the soil, and the groundwater and slowed any recovery that might otherwise have occurred when the droughts ended.

The once-great waters of the Sonoita Valley are unlikely to return. Fortunately, not all of the surface water is gone. A magnificent wetland *(cienega)* remains along the Babocomari River. A smaller cienega is protected by the Nature Conservancy in O'Donnell Canyon, a short distance upstream from the Research Ranch boundary. Impoundments in Post and O'Donnell and Lyle Canyons, including some on the Research Ranch, continue to hold water in all but the driest of times. Even a few natural springs still manage to make it to the surface. And then there are the windmills and their associated tanks. These water improvements certainly help sustain much native biological diversity.

The local ranchers have built nearly all the windmills in the valley and keep them in good repair. The irony here is inescapable, given what an earlier century's livestock probably did to the watersheds in the first place. On the Research Ranch, the sanctuary managers maintain windmills and stock tanks that attract quail, doves, deer, collared peccary, and other water-dependent wildlife. They do this not for the benefit of bird-watchers or other human visitors but to compensate at least partly for what has been lost since the days of the beaver and the pikeminnow.

Streams and cienegas are biologically rich in and of themselves, but the water plays an equal if not greater role in sustaining the diversity of trees in the Sonoita Valley. While the uplands have their oak and juniper and mesquite, the streams and riverbanks grow trees that are bigger and probably more important to wildlife. Most notable and spectacular among the riparian trees in the Sonoita Valley are cottonwood *(alamos),* sycamore *(alisos),* willow *(saúz),* velvet ash *(fresnos),* and Arizona walnut *(nogales).* Ash trees make the best firewood, or so the English say.

Duckweed bloom in a catchment basin near Ranch Headquarters after the summer monsoon

Pond water in a catchment basin near Ranch Headquarters after the summer monsoon

Shorebird at the edge of a postmonsoon pond

Riparian woodlands make up less than five percent of the landscape of the American Southwest, yet they support a disproportionate amount of biological diversity, especially of birds. Two reasons for this are immediately evident. First, the trees are large and structurally complex, and the oldest ones have hollow limbs and natural cavities that provide refuge. Second, scarcity of water normally limits the productivity of plants and insects in arid regions, but production in riparian ecosystems can be liberated from this constraint.

Readers may have perceived that we are powerfully drawn to the ecology and aesthetics of sweeping grasslands and rolling savannas in the Sonoita Valley. However, to immerse yourself into the maximum amount of biological diversity, you must get out of those dry and relatively open places. Instead, put on some mosquito repellant and hip boots and wade out into the middle of the Babocomari cienega, or walk under the towering cottonwoods along its border or into a stand of sycamores up in Lyle Canyon on the Research Ranch. If your timing is good, it will have rained recently and hard, and the streams will be flowing. You might be fortunate enough to see a Chiricahua leopard frog, a Mexican garter snake, or one of several small native fish washed downstream from a place up in the mountains that is more permanently wet. In relatively quiet waters there might be a Mexican duck and a yellowlegs or a snipe or some other sort of wetland bird. Up close there will be a water strider or a backswimmer or another of those aquatic insects that seem to fall out of the sky wherever and whenever standing water lingers. Finally, depending upon the skill of your mind's eye, you might catch the briefest glimpse of a Colorado pikeminnow, holding steady beneath an undercut bank.

The sky was as full of motion and change as the desert beneath it was monotonous and still,—and there was so much sky, more than at sea, more than anywhere else in the world. The plain was there, under one's feet, but what one saw when one looked about was that brilliant blue world of stinging air and moving cloud. Even the mountains were mere ant-hills under it. Elsewhere the sky is the roof of the world; but here the earth was the floor of the sky. The landscape one longed for when one was away, the thing all about one, the world one actually lived in, was the sky, the sky!

Willa Cather (*Death Comes to the Archbishop*, 1927)

WHEN I FIRST STARTED to photograph the southwestern landscape twenty-five years ago, the resulting images were dominated by vast expanses of blues, complemented by slivers of dun and rust land, perhaps an unconscious homage to Barnett Newman and Jules Olitski whose color-field paintings I saw for the first time in the late 1970s. For me, both the western sky and these remarkable paintings derive their power from the same source: evocation of the infinite. As a photographer, I am compelled by a passion to capture on film (or these days, on CCD pixels!) an image that somehow expresses my emotional response to a landscape: hence, in my beginning work, "earth as the floor of the sky." As a scientist, I cannot help wondering *why* the sky—and the southwestern sky in particular—has such a profound and nearly universal effect on all who stand below it, awed.

The primary reason—if reason be appropriate to understanding a deep emotional response—is the near-absence of water vapor and manmade particulates above much of the American Southwest. In the East and Midwest, and throughout northern Europe, the humidity is typically much higher and particulate matter produced by heavy industry far more prevalent. There, water molecules and tiny particles suspended in the lower atmosphere scatter sunlight, producing—even on a (rare) clear day—a haze: milky white at midday, becoming progressively ruddier toward sunset. The sky feels close and to some, even oppressive. By contrast, the scattering of sunlight from the mix of oxygen, nitrogen and other trace molecules that dominate the dry atmosphere above the Southwest produces very different hues: light blue at the horizon, gradually deepening toward the zenith. The strong color gradient creates the illusion of a dome of incomprehensible dimension, as well as the subconscious feeling that beyond the indigo atmosphere at zenith lies the darkness and infinity of space.

A secondary and related reason is greater horizontal transparency, again resulting from the relative absence of water molecules and dust particles that absorb as well as scatter light. It is not uncommon in the Southwest to have a clear view of the horizon and distant mountains, sharp and well defined at distances of up to sixty miles: the land stretching out and at the point where it curves beyond view, distinct, finite, and separate from the sky.

The coming of the rainy season in July and August alters the skyscape radically. The southeast wind carries moisture from the Gulf of Mexico, filling the air over New Mexico and Arizona with an abundance of water molecules that in aggregate on some days create a hazy "ceiling" over the Research Ranch. It is a welcome, though thankfully relatively brief, reminder of the natural,

Sky above the Canelo Hills in late spring after the April 2002 fire

seasonal "rhythm" in atmospheric circulation that brings life-giving moisture.

Sometimes, often a month or so before the onset of the rainy season, a southeast wind dips over Cananea in Sonora, Mexico, and brings with it not the much-needed moisture but instead the by-products of copper mines and smelters. For several days this circulation pattern creates a pall over southeastern Arizona, which is both unhealthy and, for confirmed westerners who have come to depend on the illusion of unlimited horizons and infinite possibilities for sustenance, spiritually depressing. These days remind us of the relative ease with which humans, acting quite rationally in a local context, can set in motion events that have unintended effects on the well-being of other humans hundreds or thousands of miles distant. We are not isolated from each other on this planet, and we are foolish when we willfully forget, and act otherwise.

At sunset, the sky over the Research Ranch transforms from the soft blue-gray of dusk to the twilight glow of the zodiacal light. Within less than an hour, the sky becomes a subliminal presence, a velvetlike black that sets off the light emanating from thousands of individual stars and, in midsummer and midwinter, from the 100 billion distant suns that constitute the disk of our Milky Way galaxy. The combination of atmospheric clarity and the relative faintness of light scattered toward Sonoita from nearby cities produces a night skyscape that finds few matches on Earth.

The dark night sky and the silence of the Sonoita Valley on a calm night compel contemplation—of the vastness of the universe beyond, of the complex series of events that led to the formation of Earth and the appearance of life, of how common or rare planets like Earth and places like the Sonoita Valley might be, and of whether we humans are alone or one of a large family of sentient beings.

The value placed on the dark skies of the Sonoita Valley is manifest in both casual conversation and formal surveys: valley residents who agree on little else find common cause in wanting to ensure that they and their children continue to enjoy the beauty and spiritual sustenance provided by the visceral connection to the universe beyond, which dark skies provide. The faint glows from the lights of Tucson on the distant northern horizon and from Sierra Vista to the east are silent but powerful reminders that the number of places on earth with truly dark skies is diminishing decade by decade and that preserving them requires collective vigilance: to shield lights and to deploy them with modesty, forethought, and concern for what might be lost through a series of seemingly benign and uncoordinated acts of carelessness.

Northeast corner of the Research Ranch, late spring

ABOUT FOURTEEN MILLION species of plants, animals, fungi, and microbes exist on the Earth. This is only an educated guess, since most of them have yet to be described or even discovered. Another educated guess is that a third of these species will go extinct before the end of the present century because of human activities. The most important human impacts are habitat loss and degradation resulting from our ever-increasing need for more of the world's natural resources, including enough space in which to fit our houses and farms and roads and shopping malls.

Does it matter if all those species disappear? Periods of mass extinction occurred in the past, long before humans came on the scene. Millions of species already have preceded us to extinction over the history of the Earth, and life went on without them as new forms evolved that replaced the old ones. That is likely to happen again, following the next great extinction. What is less likely is that humans will be around to see this process happen. Even if we do survive, the aftermath of extinction almost certainly is not going to be a good time.

On the whole, preventing the next mass extinction would seem to be a very good idea—a hard thing, perhaps, but a good thing. Ecologists, economists, and philosophers have thought and conversed at length about why we should work to protect the diversity of living things on Earth. They have come up with three different reasons, none of which necessarily trumps the others. In simplest form, the argument goes like this: We should conserve the Earth's biodiversity because

We need it.
We like it.
It is the right thing to do.

The first argument is practical. Other living species provide all our food and much of our fiber—not just the things we hunt and fish, but all the plants that feed the animals we have domesticated, and of course the crop plants themselves. A great many more species play critical support roles, providing so-called ecosystem services. They hold the soils in place. They recycle the nutrients that make our crops grow. They make water drinkable and air breathable. All of these things are true about the species that live within grasslands such as the Sonoita Valley and that help make it such a sustaining place.

The second argument for conserving biodiversity is aesthetic. Life on Earth is interesting and pleasing, substantially because of the beauty of other living things, of natural landscapes, and of relatively undisturbed and wild places. If you doubt the truth of this assertion, have a look at the pictures in this book.

The third argument is moral. It is the hardest to defend in practical terms, but to some of us it is critical. We did not create the other living things on Earth, and we have no right to cause their extinction, however inevitable that might be. This is an old precept in many of the world's religions, though perhaps not all of them.

If you ask biologists why it is important to conserve biodiversity, they are most likely to start with the first argument, because it is easiest to defend in scientific terms. But if you take the trouble to probe a little, you are likely to find that most of us are passionate about the second reason. After all, most of us became biologists because the variety of life fascinates us. We *like* other living things. We are the kids who went to school with frogs in our pockets or had the snake wriggle loose during show-and-tell. We used the pages of our history textbooks to press plants when we were supposed to be reading about the Gadsden Purchase. We got caught in the local cemetery collecting butterflies among the headstones; it seemed like such a good idea, with all those flowers around.

Recently we picked up a brochure in a Sonoita real estate office that touted the many benefits of living in the valley. First it mentioned the grasslands and the oaks, and the pronghorn and the javelina; then it got around to the schools and the neighbors, and the chance to have your own horse and to see a real cowboy. This makes us optimistic about the future of living things in the valley. Reason number two seems to work for a lot of the valley's residents, not just for a few eccentric biologists.

Defending the full variety of living things on the Earth in general, or in the Sonoita Valley in particular, is likely to rest more on aesthetics and ethics than on ecosystem science. Many of our scientific colleagues would frown at this statement, at least publicly, even though most of them probably are stealthy supporters of reason number two. They are worried because the notion minimizes the commonsense reasons to conserve species.

Add to these pragmatists the developer who has big plans for the land and the people and wishes that certain owls, for example, would fall off the edge of the Earth. The developer asks, "Aren't people more important than owls?"

We think our scientific colleagues and the developer have both got it wrong. We do absolutely depend on other living things for our material survival, and that is a good reason to con-

serve them. If we started to subtract species from the Sonoita Valley, at random and one by one, at some point the ecosystems on which we depend for grass and air and water would collapse. The science of ecology is sufficiently immature that no one can say for certain at what point during this serial extinction the collapse would occur. But long before then, the valley would have ceased to be an interesting place to live, for most of the people who live there. Both the scientist and the developer need to acknowledge the importance of this simple fact and not underestimate the importance many people attach to the aesthetics of the place they live, as well as the price they are willing to pay to preserve those aesthetic values.

The diversity of most grasslands is lower than that of most forests, first because they are simpler, essentially two-dimensional places, and second because they are relatively arid and therefore tolerable to a lesser variety of living things. However, the variety of species living in the Sonoita Valley is high compared to grasslands across the rest of North America, because the low latitude, moist summers, and relatively mild winters make it accessible and acceptable to both semitropical and temperate plants and animals. We have been disappointed in the past with the relatively scant attention that grasslands have received from individuals developing strategies for conserving the world's biodiversity. We have been gratified that so many residents of the Sonoita Valley apparently feel otherwise.

The chapters in this section are stories about biodiversity. We chose not to include stories about individual grasses or the savanna trees, because these are the big players covered in part 1. We did not select the species because they are important in material ways to human welfare, although some of them are. We chose them principally because they are part of the aesthetics of the Sonoita Valley and because they exemplify the ways to survive in a grassland or a savanna that is sometimes lush but sometimes harsh, and almost always risky. As everywhere in the natural world, something else is out there that needs the same things you do or that wants to have you for a meal. The strategies that both plants and animals have evolved to overcome these obstacles are much of what makes them both interesting and beautiful. This theme will appear repeatedly in their different stories.

PROMINENT FEATURES of the Sonoita Valley are the agave plants that punctuate the landscape like big spiny cabbages. Each year a few of them produce great tall flowering stalks. They grow best in open grasslands on hilltops and slopes. Agaves tolerate fire and drought and grazing, and their nectar is an important resource for a variety of pollinating insects, birds, and bats. Only peccaries (also known as "javelina") are tough enough to eat their fleshy leaves, although deer and cattle sometimes eat the young flowering stalks. Agaves appear to be about equally common on and off the Research Ranch, perhaps because any loss of flowers to cattle is compensated for by openings that grazing creates in the grasses, openings where the agave seeds can germinate and grow. The lesser long-nosed bat is an endangered species that depends on the nectar of agaves and other large night-blooming succulents for food. That is one very good reason not to disturb agaves in the Sonoita Valley and especially not to destroy their flowering stalks.

Agaves mostly grow wild, but people also use them in landscaping. One particular kind of agave is cultivated in Mexico, where growers harvest the extracts used to make tequila and mescal. Historically and prehistorically, Native Americans found many other uses for agave: they fashioned the tips of the leaves into needles and separated fibers (sisal) from the bodies of the leaves for threads used in sewing or ropemaking. Other useful items derived from agave include medicines, soap, and food.

Some species of agaves are called century plants, under the mistaken notion that they live about a hundred years. The two common century plants in the Sonoita Valley can live a long time, but usually only twenty-five to thirty years. The truly strange thing about century plant agaves is that they flower

and set seed only a single time in all their years, and this happens just before they die. Once reproduction begins, death inevitably follows in the same growing season. In an attempt to postpone the inevitable, gardeners may trim the flowering stalk as it begins to grow, but this does nothing to prolong the life of the plant. Like the salmon of the Pacific Northwest, the spawning agave has set itself upon an inexorable one-way journey, culminating in sex followed quickly by death.

The rules of natural selection dictate that whoever has the most surviving offspring wins the evolutionary race. Future generations inevitably are more like the parents who have given rise to many young than the parents who produced few or none. This rule is so powerful that every species has evolved the reproductive capacity to crowd the world with its own numbers in a surprisingly short time, as long as resources are abundant and enemies are scarce. Of course, such crowding rarely occurs in nature, where resources almost always become scarce and enemies usually are abundant.

Two reproductive strategies predominate among plants. By far the most common pattern is the perennial strategy, in which flowering plants live multiple years and usually produce many, many seed crops before they die. As we describe in chapter five, for example, an individual Emory oak in the Sonoita Valley can flower a hundred times or more in its lifetime and leave behind thousands of seeds. The same is true of most of the grasses. The second reproductive strategy is found in annual plants. They germinate, grow, put all their energy and resources into seeds, and then die—all in one growing season. The whole process can be telescoped into a few weeks in the Sonoran Desert, because the adult desert annuals aren't equipped to survive the scorching early

View toward Bald Hill with foreground sotol (left) and agave stalk (right)

Fire-scarred agave

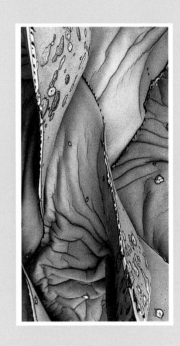

Agave leaves

Agave leaves surrounding emerging stalk

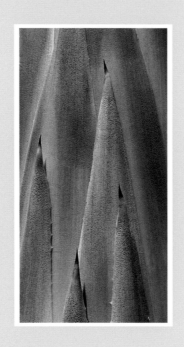

Agave leaves surrounding emerging stalk

summer drought. There are some annual plants in the Sonoita Valley, as in most habitats outside the true tropics. This suggests that a viable alternative to being perennial is to put all resources into seed production as quickly as possible and to go out in one spectacular reproductive Big Bang.

The puzzling and unusual thing about a century plant is that it lives all those years without even attempting to produce seeds, until the very end of its life. If you are going to kill yourself reproducing, why wait around so long to do it?

The same question applies to the Pacific salmon. Nothing about the upstream journey requires death: indeed, Atlantic salmon and steelhead trout of the Pacific Slope frequently turn around and go back to the ocean after they have spawned, only to return back upstream to breed again. If the Pacific salmon is going to breed only once and then die, why go to all the trouble to swim down to the ocean, cruise around for four or five years, and then swim all the way back? Why not just stay in the stream where it was born?

Why do Pacific salmon and century plants inevitably couple sexual reproduction with death, and why do they take years to get around to it? Biologists have proposed some possible explanations, although these are very different for the salmon and the agave.

The headwater streams in which Pacific salmon are born are relatively sterile places, lacking in critical nutrients that will produce the algae and insects necessary to keep the young fish growing and healthy. When the adult salmon die, their bodies decompose and fertilize the streams where they have just finished laying their eggs. Pacific salmon literally are killing themselves to make life better for their own young. Think of the salmon not as a robust marine predator that goes into freshwater to breed but as a relatively tiny fish of small streams that makes a once-in-a-life-time run to the ocean to pick up groceries for the family. And it takes more than one year to get enough groceries.

The "Big Bang" agaves are not killing themselves to feed their offspring, so there must be some other reason why they live so long before they reproduce. Biologists think this reason has to do with the energy and nutrients the agaves have accumulated over time in their fleshy green blades and in their fat stems. These storage organs enable the plants to mobilize the resources needed to produce their enormous flowering stalks and to do so in a hurry when the conditions are just right.

Because negative genetic consequences can result from inbreeding, it is helpful if the sperm and egg that combine to make a seed come from two different plants. This helps to ensure that the offspring have substantial genetic variability, and this in turn increases the likelihood that the offspring will be adaptable and viable in a wide range of environmental circumstances. Plants have an inherent disadvantage compared to animals in this regard because of their immobility. They cannot travel to find a mate but must depend on some other agent to carry sperm (pollen) from one flower to another. Everything else being equal, it is a good idea if the pollen that fertilizes the eggs comes from a distant plant, and that a plant's own pollen in turn is carried some great distance into another agave population.

The eggs in the flowers of agave plants are fertilized with pollen delivered by animals, especially bats and hummingbirds that have high energy demands and large home ranges. These animals visit the agaves for the nectar that oozes from the bases of the flowers. They facilitate agave outbreeding by carrying pollen on their bodies from one plant to another. The agave plant that produces the most nectar and puts on the biggest show doing it is likely to be the one that attracts the most hummingbirds and bats from the greatest distances. As a result, it gets fertilized by pollen from genetically unrelated individuals.

Agaves compete with one another for pollinators, and whoever has the biggest flowering stalk is most likely to win the competition. At some unknown place and time there must have been agaves genetically programmed to kill themselves growing the biggest flowering stalks possible. They won a critical reproductive contest, and the century plant evolved.

Dead agave plants are conspicuous in the Sonoita Valley. Their once-great flowering stalks stand for a while, but eventually they topple in the wind. Scattered around each parental corpse will be the offspring, contestants in the next century plant sweepstakes.

WE BELIEVE THE FOLLOWING four statements are true about snakes in the Sonoita Valley. First, the great majority of species are not venomous and pose no threat to humans. Second, snakes are beautiful and natural contributors to biological diversity in the valley, and they occupy pivotal ecological positions because of their predatory impacts on insect and rodent populations. Third, rattlesnakes rarely strike at humans, because it is a risky thing to do. Most snakebites occur when people attempt to handle the animals. Fourth, an encounter with an agitated rattlesnake almost always scares the living daylights out of a person.

Three kinds of rattlesnakes occur regularly in the Sonoita Valley—the black-tailed, the Mojave, and the western diamond-backed. Each is distinctive from the others in appearance, habitat, and temperament.

The black-tailed rattlesnake is a relatively docile animal that usually lives in the oaks and near rocky outcrops. Unlike other rattlesnakes in the valley, it lacks the alternating bands of black and white on its tail, hence its common name.

Mojave rattlesnakes have banded tails, and the rest of their bodies are mottled olive green or dull brownish-yellow. Mojaves live mostly in upland grasslands, and they have particularly toxic venom.

The western diamond-backed rattlesnake is by far the largest of the three, and the most aggressive. Diamond-backs mostly occupy shrubby and rocky washes and, especially, floodplains with sacaton grass, where they like to eat cotton rats. They have banded tails and a general salt-and-pepper sort of look, along with diamond-shaped markings on their backs. It is easy to walk right past a black-tail or a Mojave without the snake ever moving, let alone rattling, whereas diamond-backeds almost always rear up into the characteristic defensive pose and give the full sound-effects treatment, which includes both a tail rattle and a muffled hiss.

We have been told that diamond-backed rattlesnakes have become relatively silent in places such as Florida and Texas, where humans regularly and enthusiastically persecute them. It could be that they have learned to keep quiet, but more likely this is a case of evolution. In rattlesnake-roundup country, it is the silent snake that lives to pass on a genetic predisposition toward keeping still. Noisy rattlesnakes end up as belts and hatbands and as the subjects of stories in saloons.

Rattlesnakes are more likely to live near human habitations than would be the case if they crawled around at random, for two reasons. First, they mostly hunt mice, some kinds of which are attracted to houses and yards because of increased water and food. Second, rattlesnakes cannot climb, and so when they encounter an obstacle in their paths they will travel along its edge, looking for a way around. This is called drifting. If the edge happens to be a wall, the snake will drift until it comes to a corner. If it happens to be an outside corner, the snake turns and keeps going. But if it is an inside corner—for example, in an alcove by the front door or in the back of the garage—the snake is likely to curl up and wait for prey in a place it perceives to be relatively safe.

A person walking along the side of a road crossing the Sonoita Valley is more likely to be run down by a pickup truck than to be bitten by a rattlesnake. Why, then, are rattlesnakes more frightening than pickup trucks? We think it is because

Western diamond-backed rattlesnake (photo by Greg Joder)   *Cotton rat*

rattlesnakes have evolved to be scary, and humans in turn have evolved to be scared. It is a mutually adaptive relationship.

In our personal experience the human fright response to a snake is deep, nearly subconscious, and virtually unstoppable. It has little or nothing to do with any religious or psychological notions about what the snakes represent symbolically. Rattlesnakes don't symbolize danger: they are danger. Yet, and this is a key point, the danger is easily avoided because it is in the best interest of both parties for that to happen. A snake will strike defensively only as a last resort, because it will have wasted its venom on something that is not food and because there is a high probability that it will be killed or injured as a result of that behavior.

A popular format for televised nature programs is to have someone grab a highly poisonous snake by the tail and hold it up for the audience to admire, while proclaiming both its beauty and the fact that it is something like the third most venomous viper known to exist. The snake all the while is attempting to twist around and bite the "naturalist" on the nose. There is little doubt that this possibility has much to do with the popularity of these programs. The opportunity to watch natural selection in action is something most people don't want to miss, even those who profess not to believe in evolution.

Given a natural and adaptive fear of poisonous snakes, it is hard for many people to find them interesting, let alone admirable. Yet it is easy for most biologists, who are intrigued by rattlesnakes because of their abilities as well as their limitations.

Rattlesnakes are extraordinary predators. Their keen olfactory organs and the heat-sensitive pits between each eye and nostril allow them to find and track their prey. Their hollow and movable fangs swing out during the strike, puncturing and poisoning the victim in an instant. The snake then immediately draws back to safety and waits for the venom to take effect before attempting to swallow the prey. If the mouse or rat crawls away, the snake is able to track it by scent. Laboratory experiments have shown that a rattlesnake can distinguish the odor of a mouse it has just struck from that of another individual, so it will not accidentally follow the trail left by a different animal.

Because rattlesnakes are ectotherms (or "cold-blooded"), they must find warm, secure, and secluded places to spend the winter in the Sonoita Valley. Often such underground dens are the traditional wintering places for many individuals, in part because the extra bodies mean more heat. When spring comes the snakes leave their hiding places and spread out across the valley in search of good prey populations. Rattlesnakes use the position of the sun and the stars to navigate their way back to the den in the fall, just like migrating birds and sea turtles. They also use their own scent trails as guides during the return journey.

The daily activities of rattlesnakes in summer are dependent on the weather. Snakes cannot tolerate direct exposure to the heat of the sun, nor can they function well on clear, cool nights.

Daytime encounters with rattlesnakes are much more likely after the start of the summer monsoon, because the cloud cover provides critical shade. Nighttime encounters with rattlesnakes frequently occur on roads, because the snakes have crawled out there to absorb heat stored in the pavement, which is still warm from the previous day's exposure to the sun.

Despite their specializations and abilities, and perhaps in part because of them, rattlesnakes have significant behavioral limitations. The relatively heavy bodies of rattlesnakes are capable of delivering the fangs and their deadly content with extraordinary speed and precision, but in others ways these reptiles are rather cumbersome animals. They cannot climb into or over anything higher than about one-half or even one-third of their body lengths. They travel relatively slowly compared to much more agile nonvenomous snakes in the valley such as the Sonoran whipsnake. Rattlesnakes are among the very few kinds of animals that suffer significant mortality during fire, because they are too slow to get out of the way. On more than one occasion, we have observed a rattlesnake rear up in a threatening pose, only to topple over backward down the hill. It is hard not to imagine that they are embarrassed when this happens, since the end of the fall is followed by much coiling and rattling and generally aggressive posturing.

THE BIRD FAMILY CORVIDAE includes crows, ravens, nutcrackers, and jays. Corvids as a group are intelligent and social, compared to most other sorts of birds. These characteristics may be linked, since a social life can take considerable brainpower. One example is the gang of Chihuahuan ravens that hang around the Santa Cruz County landfill, just east of Sonoita. We have the impression that it takes about five minutes for every raven in the valley to get the word when a particularly juicy load of garbage has been dropped off.

Among all corvids in North America, none has a more complicated social life than the Mexican jay. Flocks of these gray-and-sky-blue birds inhabit the oak woodlands that surround the Sonoita Valley. They adapt well to humans and they like bird feeders, so the jays are familiar to nearly every human resident. Mexican jays live year-round in tight social groups of five to a dozen or more individuals. In late summer and fall, they harvest acorns from the oaks, bury them by the hundreds or thousands in the ground on their territories, and then live through the winter largely by digging up the acorns and eating them. Mexican jays have remarkable memories for the places where they have buried acorns. However, in bumper-crop years they will bury more acorns than they need to get through the winter. These forgotten acorns are the ones that can grow up to be part of the next generation of oaks.

In spring, several males in a particular group of Mexican jays will start to build separate nests, to which each attracts (or tries to attract) an individual female with whom he will mate. Eventually, two or three or even four nests will have eggs and young. Once the eggs hatch, nearly all the birds in the flock, whether or not they are the parents, help feed the young from all of the nests. This apparent altruism on the part of many Mexican jays initially puzzled biologists, until they learned that the flocks actually are large extended families. When a jay is feeding somebody else's young, the nestlings most likely are nieces, nephews, cousins, brothers, sisters, or even grandchildren. It is adaptive in an evolutionary sense to raise younger relatives, because they share many genes.

Mexican jays are loud and boisterous, especially outside the nesting season when the flocks are moving together among the oaks, from one acorn cache to the next. They give every indication of being in charge on their territories: familiar with the terrain, going where they want and when they want, and being generally intolerant of, or at least oblivious to, other birds. Yet over the years we have noticed a peculiar thing. Repeatedly, except during the nesting season, flocks of Mexican jays did not travel alone on the Research Ranch. Instead, they were attended by one or a few individuals of another species—the northern flicker. Why might this have been the case? Was it just a coincidence? Were the jays and flickers aggressive toward one another? Were flickers attempting to rob the jays' acorns? When a flock moved, which species took the lead and which followed? Did any other species associate with the jay flocks besides flickers?

The northern flicker is a kind of woodpecker that (like the other members of its family) nests in hollow tree cavities. Unlike most other woodpeckers, flickers feed mainly on the ground, where they dig and probe, especially for ants. At the right season they also will eat a variety of fruits and seeds, but they are not known to have any particular affinity for acorns. Flickers are modestly colored in brown and gray, except for some red and

Multilevel oak savanna landscape, view from East Mesa

black head markings and distinctive brightly colored underwings that flash during flight.

Birds are thought to flock together outside the nesting season for one or both of two very different adaptive reasons. The first has to do with finding food. Suppose a flicker is feeding on the ground looking for ants but is unable to find any. It is time to move and look somewhere else. Instead of looking for ants, which are hard to see from a distance, it might look for another flicker. If birds use one another as clues to good feeding spots, then flocks will form automatically. The second reason for flocking has to do with security from predators. If a flicker is feeding alone on the ground, busily digging for ants, it might not see the hawk circling overhead in time to avoid becoming prey. If it is feeding near two or three other birds, the odds improve that somebody will see the hawk coming.

For which of these two reasons (finding food, avoiding predators) might flickers have associated with flocks of Mexican jays? Both are plausible. Flickers feed on the ground, and they might follow jays with the expectation that the other birds would give away the locations of buried acorns, which the flickers then could unearth. Alternatively, the flickers might choose to dig for ants while mixed with a flock of jays looking for acorns, to decrease the chances that a predator might catch them by surprise.

Extended field observations revealed more precisely what was going on between flickers and Mexican jays. In fall and winter, but not during the nesting season, flickers and jays were together far more often than could be attributed to chance. When the jays moved, the flickers followed. Yet flickers never attempted to dig up the jays' buried acorns. Instead they dug for ants while the jays caught other sorts of insects, mostly grasshoppers, as well as digging up acorns. No aggression between the two kinds of birds appeared to occur; the atmosphere was all very placid and quiet, except when hawks flew into view.

Cooper's hawks are avian predators that reside year-round in the oak savannas of southeastern Arizona. These are agile birds whose usual hunting strategy is to fly fast and low through the trees and across the open grasslands in hopes of surprising any of a variety of small and medium-sized birds before they have a chance to flee. Cooper's hawks take captured prey to a log or some other convenient horizontal surface, where they pluck it before eating the meat or sharing it with a mate or nestling. Plucking stations can be littered with feathers (and sometimes fur) from past kills. It is not uncommon to see both flicker and jay feathers around Cooper's hawk plucking stations, which gives some quantitative indication of why it pays for Mexican jays to be social and for flickers to tag along.

Why don't all jays and flickers eventually fall prey to Cooper's hawks? In part it is because Mexican jays post sentries. While most members of a flock are feeding on the ground, with their backs to the sky, one bird almost inevitably sits alone atop a nearby oak. When a hawk flies into view, the sentry sounds an alarm and all the birds fly into the sheltering canopy of the oak.

Given the efficiency of the jay sentry system and all those pairs of eyes on the watch for predators, it might seem a wonder that the hawks ever succeed. Yet the hawks clearly do win out some of the time, as the plucking stations attest. We have seen jays and especially flickers lag behind after the rest of the flock has moved on. Perhaps they just unearthed an acorn or a rich nest of ants that was too good to pass up. Sometimes this must be a fatal mistake.

In the case of the Mexican jay, there is no such thing as having too many eyes on the lookout, and apparently it is more than all right if some of them are flicker eyes. Mexican jays and northern flickers are thus two otherwise very different birds that are united by having a common predatory enemy.

PALEONTOLOGISTS STUDY the history of life on earth, attempting to learn who evolved from whom and when, mostly by examining fossils and the attributes of living forms. Paleoecologists wish to understand how species interacted with one another and assembled themselves into biological communities, in ancient times. This is a difficult task, sometimes based on scant evidence. Which species are found in the same fossil beds, and does that mean they were together at the exact same moments in history? From petrified feces, what were the diets of prehistoric predators and herbivores? Which species were common in ancient times, and which were relatively rare?

Paleoecological data are important to biologists for at least two reasons. First, they tell us about past environments. Second, they give us clues to the ecological conditions under which species evolved that are still with us today. Paleobiologists often are critical of ecologists who study contemporary biological communities and try to interpret relationships among the various species without regard for their evolutionary histories. It is a fair criticism, but the problem usually is a scarcity of paleoecological data. What biologists attempt as an alternative is to obtain clues about the past of a species by observing how it reacts to a range of modern environments and to the other plants and animals with which it lives. For example, if ecologists wanted to understand the historical impacts of livestock grazing in the Sonoita Valley, they might study those species remaining today that show a strong preference for tall and dense grass cover and that become scarce when a grassland is heavily grazed. Native vertebrate animals in this category include the bunchgrass lizard, Montezuma quail, Botteri's sparrow, Cassin's sparrow, grasshopper sparrow,

pygmy mouse, and three species of cotton rats. The Botteri's sparrow has been one of those most affected by grazing historically, and therefore it is a prime test subject. What can it tell us, by means of its ecology and behavior, about the nature of Sonoita Valley grasslands as they appeared before the introduction of domestic grazers?

The Botteri's sparrow is an obscure brown bird that spends most of its time hidden in the grass and that has almost no distinctive attributes even when it happens to sit up where an ecologist or an ornithologist can see it. The males have a distinctive song—a series of simple notes given at increasing frequency, like a ping-pong ball bouncing to rest. Otherwise, little distinguishes the Botteri's sparrow physically from a dozen of its relatives or, for that matter, from a sparrow-shaped chunk of adobe. Yet the Botteri's sparrow has a story to tell, and we have spent much of the past thirty years attempting to figure out what it is trying to tell us about grasslands in the Sonoita Valley.

The Botteri's sparrow is largely a bird of Mexico whose breeding range extends north into extreme southeastern Arizona and the south Texas coastal plain. The bird was known to early Arizona ornithologists, but it apparently disappeared from the state in the early 1900s and was not seen again until 1932. By the 1980s it had become a common bird on the Research Ranch and elsewhere in the Sonoita Valley where the grass cover was sufficient.

Botteri's sparrows are monogamous, usually producing only one brood of young per year, and in most ways their reproductive cycle is absolutely unremarkable. They have a strong tendency to return to breed on the same territories in subsequent years, but this sort of site fidelity (called "philopatry") is common among

Botteri's sparrow

Left to right: Sacaton grass, Sideoats grama, Boer lovegrass

birds. If there is one unusual aspect to the breeding biology of the Botteri's sparrow, it is the rapidity with which nestlings are fledged—at a mere ten days after hatching. The young sparrows can scarcely fly at first, and they are dependent upon their parents for protection and food for up to a month after they leave the nest. This postfledging period may be critical for Botteri's sparrows, and it may explain their distinctive habitat needs.

When we first studied Botteri's sparrows at the Research Ranch in the 1980s, most of the birds appeared to be associated with sacaton, the unusually tall grass that mostly grows in floodplains (see chapter three). This finding was consistent with the widely held view that the Botteri's sparrow is a southwestern tallgrass specialist. Sacaton bottomlands suffered grievously from

drought, overgrazing, and streambed channelization in the late 1890s in Arizona, which certainly might explain the sparrow's disappearance from the state shortly thereafter. Another aspect to the breeding biology of the Botteri's sparrow, the early fledging time, suggests an evolutionary link to sacaton. Sacaton bottomlands can flood during the summer monsoon, and we have seen nests and nestlings washed away during such events on the Research Ranch. Young birds out of the nest would have a much better chance to escape flooding, even if they cannot yet fly.

In the late 1980s our impression of the Botteri's sparrow as a sacaton specialist began to change drastically because it had started to become common in another sort of grassland. Although the overall goal of the sanctuary is to provide opportunities for native

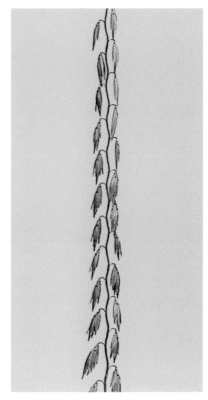

flora and fauna, two exotic grasses native to southern Africa dominate some parts of the property. Lehmann lovegrass and Boer lovegrass are hardy and prolific species that ranchers and range managers purposefully introduced into the Southwest in the 1930s and 1940s as a means of restoring degraded rangelands. These grasses have since spread over hundreds of thousands of acres in the region, including two major areas on the Research Ranch, generally at the expense of native grasses and wild-flowers (see chapter thirteen). We have learned that these near-monocultures of exotic lovegrasses are attractive to relatively few birds, mammals, or insects. A conspicuous exception is the Botteri's sparrow, which in our surveys seemed to be the most common bird out there. Why might stands of nonnative

grass attract this sparrow, which otherwise seemed to be a habitat specialist?

In 1999, we initiated a study of Botteri's sparrows on the Research Ranch. The goals of this study were to quantify the abundance, reproductive success, and site fidelity of the populations of this species in three different grasslands on the sanctuary: sacaton floodplains, stands of the exotic African lovegrasses, and upland areas dominated by native grasses other than sacaton. We entered this study with three related observations, or at least impressions, already in hand. First, the birds seemed most abundant in sacaton, intermediate in the exotic lovegrasses, and least common in upland native grasslands. Second, the three habitats ranked in the same order from most to least grass cover. Third, plantations of the African exotics, especially Boer lovegrass, looked like sacaton stands in terms of uniformity and density, although they were only about half as tall.

It seemed clear to us that Botteri's sparrows were attracted to Boer lovegrass stands, probably because they were similar in some critical way to sacaton. But was this a good thing for the sparrows? Did the exotic plantations represent a new ecological opportunity, or were they an ecological trap, superficially resembling sacaton but perhaps lacking in critical food or other resources? We knew from earlier work that the exotic grasslands supported relatively few insects, probably because of the lower variety of plant life compared to areas dominated by native vegetation. If insect food was limiting to the reproductive success of the Botteri's sparrow, then the attractiveness of Boer lovegrass might prove to be a cruel illusion. However, many studies have shown that songbird reproductive success is less a matter of the parents delivering sufficient food than it is of the nest remaining undetected by predators—and if the latter mattered the most, then the heavy cover of the robust African exotic grasses might be perfect.

The results of the study were clear but complex. As we predicted, nesting densities on the Research Ranch were highest in sacaton, intermediate in the exotics, and lowest in native upland grasslands. Site fidelity—the numbers of birds color-banded in 1999 and 2000 that returned to their previously held territories in 2000 and 2001—was about equally high in sacaton and exotics but somewhat lower in native uplands. We found 314 nests during the three summers. To our surprise, their success did not differ among the three habitats, in terms of either the frequency of predation or the number of young fledged per nest that escaped predation.

Why did Botteri's sparrows prefer sacaton and to a lesser extent the exotic grasses, if the grass type did not matter to nesting success? We cannot be certain, but one explanation has to do with where the parent birds preferred to stash recently fledged young during the critical period just after the fledglings leave the nest and before they can fly well enough to escape predation. Although there was no easy way to measure the survival rates of young birds, we could measure the cover around places where parents hid their young and then compare the availability of this sort of cover in the three habitats. When we did this, a clear pattern emerged. In sacaton, nearly the whole stand had sufficient cover. In the exotic grasslands, lots of places did. But patches of heavy cover were relatively scarce in the native upland grasslands. In sacaton, a gopher snake or northern mockingbird or coyote would not know where to begin looking for a young Botteri's sparrow. In native upland grasslands, there would be relatively few such places where a young sparrow could hide, and they would be much more obvious. The hunting would be easy.

One puzzle remains. If protective cover was greater in sacaton, then why were Botteri's sparrow nests as likely to be lost to predation there as in the other grasslands? Why did cover matter only after the young had fledged? These are good and difficult questions, which we attempted to answer at least in part by measuring vegetative cover around nests as well as fledglings. What we found was that the parents were much less selective about nest placement than they were about hiding their fledged young. Almost any sort of grass clump or shrub would do for a nest, but much more extensive cover was needed, or at least sought out, for a young bird. For reasons we do not fully understand, it seems clear that fledgling cover is more important than nesting cover for

Botteri's sparrows. If this pattern has any generality among birds, the lesson for avian ecologists is that we should be including fledgling as well as nest locations in assessing the quality of any particular habitat for any particular bird species.

The reader might legitimately ask what any of this has to do with paleoecology, which is where this chapter began. There is a clear link. Ultimately, what we most wanted to learn about the Botteri's sparrow is what it thinks (in an evolutionary sense) are the best places to live and reproduce. What sorts of grasslands did it select for breeding in the Sonoita Valley in the year 1492, or 5,000 years before then, and why? In all likelihood it still uses those same genetic memories today in deciding where and when to build a nest, even though the grasslands in the valley have been substantially rearranged.

In the eye of the Botteri's sparrow, what does the Sonoita Valley *look* like? One possibility is that these birds are searching for sacaton, or something like it, and always have been. By this scenario, the species has always been a relatively uncommon tall-grass specialist, restricted to only a few places north of Mexico. Another possibility, and one that intrigues us, is that the Botteri's sparrow is in fact a habitat generalist, able to successfully occupy almost any sort of grassland with sufficient cover. Perhaps before the great destruction of southwestern grasslands in the late 1800s Botteri's sparrows were common in uplands as well as sacaton floodplains, and their apparent restriction to sacaton habitat prior to the introduction of the African lovegrasses is a historic artifact. In the eye of the sparrow, could those places in the Sonoita Valley that are dominated by Lehmann and Boer lovegrass look like the grasslands of two centuries before?

Clearly, the Botteri's sparrow is on the cusp of an ecological and evolutionary breakout. In less than three human generations it has gone from a species that was locally distributed and rare, to one that is wide ranging and abundant. Botteri's sparrows remain uncommon in native upland grasslands, especially those in which livestock grazing or fire has reduced cover. But the spread and dominance of relatively lush African exotics are providing an ever-increasing opportunity. We may never know if this transition represents something novel for the Botteri's sparrow, or whether it is only a return to some former glory.

THE GRASSLANDS AND SAVANNAS of North America once supported a fauna of large mammals rivaling that of east Africa. It is not fanciful to envision the Sonoita Valley of 15,000 years ago with elephants, camels, lions, cheetahs, and a host of hooved grazers including horses and bison. Notable among this prehistoric bestiary was a diverse group of relatively fleet and delicate grazers, members of the family Antilocapridae, that superficially resemble modern African antelope.

Most of the big mammals went extinct in North America by the close of the Pleistocene Epoch, about 10,000 years ago. Gone are the elephants, the native horses, and the camels, as well as all of the Antilocapridae that ever existed, save one—the pronghorn. Pronghorn and modern bison are the two most abundant North American grassland hooved mammals that survived the Pleistocene extinctions. No fossil evidence suggests that bison persisted in southeastern Arizona. Unlike bison, however, pronghorn continued to populate the region, and a particular subspecies, the Mexican pronghorn, was here to greet the first Europeans who visited the Sonoita Valley.

Thirty to sixty million pronghorn may have lived in western North America at the time of Columbus—in steppes, prairies, grass-shrublands, and even deserts—from southern Canada to northeastern Mexico and from the Pacific Coast to the eastern limits of the Great Plains. They were in for a rough time. By the early 1900s a combination of hunting, fencing, overgrazing, livestock-transmitted disease, altered fire regimes, and tilled agriculture had reduced the total pronghorn population to fewer than fifteen thousand animals. Subsequently the population recovered to more than one million, thanks to the implementa-

tion of hunting regulations and habitat improvements that have included moderation of livestock densities. The Mexican pronghorn was extirpated from Arizona by about 1920, but today there is a healthy herd in the Sonoita Valley, descended from animals brought into Arizona from Texas in the 1980s. Pronghorn have become much more common on the Research Ranch since the Ryan Fire, almost certainly because of the increase in herbaceous plants that are their preferred foods (see chapter two).

The pronghorn is particularly adapted to wide-open spaces without physical or visual barriers. In these sorts of places there is a premium on spotting a predator a long way off and then being able to outrun it if an attack comes. Pronghorn also evolved in landscapes where bison frequently were the dominant grazing animals. These evolutionary legacies both equipped and handicapped pronghorn for their subsequent encounters with humans. On the positive side of the ledger, they pretty much left the grass to bison, preferring instead to feed on other kinds of broad-leaved herbaceous plants and to a lesser degree on shrubs. As a result, they can coexist successfully with domestic livestock, as long as the grazing is not too heavy. On the negative side, pronghorn can have a terrible time with fences, because they are built to run but not to jump. Their prehistoric world contained little or nothing that required jumping over, but lots of things to run away from.

A pronghorn streaking across the prairie will either stop at a fence or attempt to slide under it, usually at high speed. The sliding strategy works if the bottom strand of the fence is not too close to the ground and especially if it is not barbed wire. Unfortunately, most fences on western ranches are all barbed

Pronghorn

wire, and they tend to be strung close to the ground because that is what keeps the calves with their mothers, and the sheep in at all. Managers at the Research Ranch (in cooperation with neighboring ranchers) have removed the bottom strands of barbed wire from boundary fences surrounding the sanctuary and have replaced them with smooth wire at least eighteen inches off the ground.

Three lines of evidence suggest that predation has been a powerful force shaping the morphology and behavior of pronghorn. First, they are highly social year-round. Both sexes and all ages aggregate into sizeable herds in winter, while female harems assemble around individual territorial males during the breeding season of spring and summer. Under either circumstance a poten-

tial advantage is that of mutual detection and defense against predators, particularly for the protection of young. However, no evidence for any such cooperation has been identified inside pronghorn groups, where most interactions are competitive and aggressive. Why then do pronghorn aggregate? The most likely explanation resides in the concept of the "selfish herd," whereby an individual animal reduces the likelihood of predation simply by mixing with others. A single pronghorn spotted by a hungry predator is almost certain to be attacked. A single pronghorn in a group of two is at half the risk, while one animal in a herd of ten has a ninety percent probability of seeing the next sunrise.

A second antipredator attribute of pronghorn is their extraordinary vision. They have very large eyes in relation to their skull and overall body size, and the eyes are placed laterally on the head, which increases peripheral vision.

Gregariousness and vision certainly are important antipredator attributes of the pronghorn, but speed is what sets this animal apart from other hooved mammals. Pronghorn can run flat-out at nearly sixty miles per hour and do it for extended periods. All such adaptations must come at some cost and compromise, however, and the more extreme the adaptation the more costly it is likely to be. In the case of the pronghorn, extra calories and materials are required to build and maintain the bones, muscles, heart, and lungs that enable the animal to achieve such astonishing speed. Also, the skeletal and associated muscle arrangements that make it easy for them to run so fast also make it very difficult for them to jump.

Pronghorn are by far the fastest New World land animals. The question is, what are they running away from? No living North American predator comes close to being able to run down an adult pronghorn. Students of pronghorn evolution and behavior believe they have found the answer, which goes back to those Pleistocene extinctions culminating 10,000 years ago. Before that time there were a variety of predators in the grasslands that apparently had a chance to catch pronghorn. Most notable among these were two species of cheetahs. Cheetahs are the fastest land animals alive, but today they survive only in the Old World. It seems that pronghorn have retained an astounding running speed that they evolved long ago in response to what have been called the ghosts of predators past. It is possible that pronghorn might eventually lose their speed, now that selection for it has abated. But 10,000 years is only an instant in evolutionary time.

Pronghorn may not be the only residents of the Sonoita Valley that are running away from the past, but they certainly are the fastest.

What is a weed? A plant whose virtues have not yet been discovered.

Ralph Waldo Emerson (1878)

THE PRICKLEPOPPY IS A TALL, bristly plant, common in the Sonoita Valley and throughout much of the arid American West. It has a large flower with delicate crinkled white petals and a cluster of bright golden anthers at the center. The foliage is gray-green and blue-green and densely covered with spines. The pricklepoppy is native to North America, by which biologists mean that it evolved here or dispersed here by itself a long time ago. This designation contrasts it with other species, called exotics or aliens, that humans have introduced either accidentally or intentionally.

Pricklepoppies are tough plants, tolerant of drought, and particularly well suited to grow in disturbed places such as roadsides or along washes. When most of the Sonoita Valley is parched brown by the annual drought of spring and early summer, lots of pricklepoppies already are growing and reproducing. We find them both admirable and beautiful.

Two pages are reserved for the pricklepoppy in Kittie F. Parker's *Illustrated Guide to Arizona Weeds*. The implication is that these plants have done something wrong—that they have failed Emerson's test for virtues. According to Parker, pricklepoppies "come in abundance on overgrazed ranges, and are an indication of severe deterioration." Apparently one of the pricklepoppy's vices is to remind us when we have done a poor job of caring for the land, and it is true that they are less common on the Research Ranch than in some other, more-disturbed parts of the Sonoita Valley. However, another view is that pricklepoppies bravely grow in otherwise bare places when all the other plants have given up. This might even qualify as a virtue.

A better definition than Emerson's posits a weed as any plant growing where it is not wanted. We like this premise because it makes the term a purely anthropocentric opinion rather than a comment about a plant's intrinsic shortcomings. It also is context-specific, because the same kind of plant might be a weed in one place and not in another. Tidy flower beds and smooth lawns on which to roll golf balls both require lots of weeding, but maintaining these sorts of places has almost nothing to do with conservation.

Most species of weeds are of little environmental concern, because they do not become common enough to threaten the function of relatively natural ecosystems or the other species living in them. However, a small number of very conspicuous exceptions can be real trouble.

Weeds that take over landscapes to the exclusion of native biodiversity are called invasives. Some of them are native plants such as the pricklepoppy, in which cases human activities almost always have created conditions where the newly anointed weed increases its range and density to the exclusion of other species. Another good example is the mesquite, a native southwestern tree discussed in chapter five. Mesquites once were common along washes and river bottoms, where they sometimes formed impressive gallery forests rich in native biodiversity. Within historic time they began to spread into grasslands, usually coincident with the introduction of domestic grazers and with reductions in fire. Mesquite and other shrubs now have so thoroughly invaded certain southwestern landscapes that they scarcely could be called grasslands at all. But this usually has not been the case in the

Pricklepoppy

Sonoita Valley, where in most places mesquite has spread into grasslands but not to the apparent detriment of the grassland flora and fauna. At least on the Research Ranch, the mesquite is not a weed.

Unlike pricklepoppies and mesquite, most successful invasive species are nonnative exotics. They may take advantage of opportunities created by human disturbances, but they have the additional advantage of having been imported without the herbivores and diseases that held them in check in their native ranges. In the Sonoita Valley, the most successful exotic invaders are two species of lovegrasses brought to the Southwest from southern Africa. Boer and Lehmann lovegrass were intentionally introduced into southeastern Arizona beginning in the 1930s, as a means of restoring native grasslands degraded by drought and livestock grazing. The introductions were all too successful, so that now there are places where almost no native grass remains. Relatively few of the native grassland animals find stands of the exotic lovegrasses acceptable, and even livestock much prefer the native forage.

Although new stands of the exotic lovegrasses are most likely to appear along roadsides or in other disturbed places, they soon begin to spread into the adjacent grasslands, even those dominated by sizeable populations of the native species. Another factor that makes these African aliens a conservation challenge is that they are almost perfect ecological mimics of the native grasses, only better. They grow in the warmest time of the year, just like the natives. They are perennial bunchgrasses, just like the natives. They thrive on fire, perhaps even better than the natives. Unlike the natives, they produce an abundance of viable seed almost every year and quickly come to dominate soil seed banks. This

means that after the next big disturbance there will be even more exotic grasses than before and even less native biodiversity.

In the 1940s or early 1950s, someone planted Boer and Lehmann lovegrass on two mesas that are part of what is now the Research Ranch. The African exotics have remained, and they support a much-reduced variety of native plants and animals compared to the rest of the sanctuary. Lehmann lovegrass in particular has spread beyond the area of the original plantings, and it represents a long-term and serious threat to the biodiversity of the property. Disturbances such as the Ryan Fire seem to have encouraged the spread.

In the beginning, range managers expressed a lot of enthusiasm for the African lovegrasses, which converted back into grasslands some places that were well on the way to becoming relatively barren desert scrub. Most of that enthusiasm is long gone. In some places, Lehmann and Boer lovegrass do support more livestock than did the exhausted native grasses they replaced. Yet the ranchers we know would gladly replace the exotic lovegrasses with healthy stands of the natives, if only they knew how to do it. By almost anybody's definition, and certainly for anyone interested in the conservation of native biodiversity, the African lovegrasses have become two of Arizona's most successful and frightening weeds.

There are thoughtful biologists and land managers who believe the threat of invasive exotic species is overblown. They point to the fact that competitively superior species have been replacing those less fit since the beginning of life on Earth. What is wrong with a newly formed southwestern grassland being dominated by two species introduced from Africa? By evidence of their own success, Lehmann and Boer lovegrass are at least as well

Lehmann lovegrass

suited to the climate and soils of southeastern Arizona as are the so-called native species. And if they happen to have escaped the ravages of herbivores and pathogens left back in Africa, well, so much the better for local grassland productivity. Eventually they might have gotten here by themselves, as seeds blown into the stratosphere by a fluke storm or stuck to the legs of a wandering bird. Probably it was only a matter of time.

However, the problem with invasive exotics *is* the matter of time. By their activities, humans now are redistributing species around the globe at rates not seen before. Although most of these introductions will fail or prove to be ecologically trivial, some few will succeed in abundance. There are two problems with this potential success. First, many of the world's widely separated and

formerly distinctive ecosystems will come to be crowded by the same few species, before the native species in any of them has time to respond. Second, if Sonoita Valley grasslands are at all typical, each individual ecosystem will contain many fewer species after a successful alien invasion. The net result is the loss of biological diversity, from local to global scales.

The threats of exotic invaders to native biodiversity almost certainly are nonlinear. By this we mean that thresholds are involved—critical points at which the invaders become so common that they threaten the survival of native species. For all of the reasons described in the introduction to part 2 of this book, we believe such losses of diversity are a very bad thing. It is critical to monitor the spread of exotics such as the African lovegrasses, to learn about their ecological limits, and then to avoid wasting time defending places that are not threatened. It is even more important to find new methods for controlling the spread of exotics, besides the risky and rarely successful use of pesticides. We see no area of environmental research toward which young conservation biologists could more profitably turn their creative energies.

Three of the most successful alien invaders of the Sonoita Valley evolved in Africa: Lehmann lovegrass, Boer lovegrass, and *Homo sapiens.* A fourth species, the cow, came from central Asia. While each has significantly altered environmental conditions, so far none of them has pushed all of the grasslands or savannas or riparian woodlands or wetlands beyond the point of recognition. That is the main reason why the valley remains such a wonderful place for people to live, and why a large proportion of its native biological diversity can still find a way to live here with us.

THE SUMMER OF 2001 started out unusually green in the Sonoita Valley. We arrived for our field season on a hot clear day in May, and the hills already looked like it was early July. But the monsoon hadn't started, and nobody was talking about much in the way of spring rain. Why, then, was the landscape so verdant?

One thing led to another that day, with unpacking and settling in and all, and we didn't have time to get out into the field. That night we ran into a rancher at a local restaurant. This particular individual is blessed with two attributes essential for anybody trying to survive by growing cattle in the New Millennium—a keen eye for the natural world, and a sense of humor.

"Well, I finally did it," he said. "You and those other short-pants boys out at the Research Ranch were right all along. The cows have killed all my grass. There's nothing left out there but a bunch of weeds."

We felt the legs of our short pants being pulled. "What?" we asked. "Then why is it so green?"

"Maybe you ought to go take a look," he said.

Our rancher friend was right, and he was right to be worried. All that green stuff turned out to be relatively little grass and mostly the young shoots of a variety of broad-leaved herbaceous plants, the kind that ranchers and range managers usually call "forbs." This is not an especially meaningful term botanically, because a forb is defined only by what it is not—as in "not grass" and "not good for my livestock."

We discovered several interesting and important things when those forbs got around to flowering later in the summer. First, most of them were members of the aster family, with common names such as goldeneye, yellow aster, purple aster, and cudweed. Second, they had such an early start and grew with such vigor throughout the summer that they actually suppressed the growth of many of the native grasses. The grama grasses in particular seemed unable to do much growing at all, trapped as they were under a canopy of forbs. And the asters and their relatives were at least as common on the Research Ranch as on adjacent land, so the great forb explosion of 2001 seemed to have little or nothing to do with grazing. Our rancher friend and his livestock may have been the victims, but they were not the cause.

By the middle of August 2001, the hills and mesas of the Sonoita Valley had turned into a mosaic of purple and white and mostly yellow, and they stayed that way until the killing frosts of November. What caused the forbs to so nearly dominate the grasses in that particular year?

Strong circumstantial evidence ties the occurrence to unusually heavy rains the previous fall. An advantage to studying one place for a long time is that relatively rare events begin to repeat themselves. We looked back at some of our data from the early 1980s on canopy cover of grasses versus forbs on the Research Ranch. In only one other summer, 1984, had the forb cover even come close to that of 2001. We next compared monthly weather data from the ranch, and discovered that the fall of 1983 was second only to the fall of 2000 in terms of precipitation.

Our working hypothesis about Sonoita Valley aster events is that they occur when seeds germinate in the spring following an unusually wet fall or winter. The plants apparently begin to grow right away, thereby gaining a competitive advantage over the native perennial grasses that wait for onset of the summer monsoon. Mass bloomings of wildflowers are known to follow wet

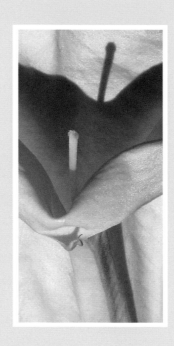

Jimsonweed

Rainbow cactus flower

Arizona mariposa lily

Mexican gold-poppy

winters in the lowlands of the Southwest, which is the reason tourists are able to predict the years when a spring trip to the desert is likely to be especially rewarding. Two things appear to be different about blooms of the asters and their relatives at higher elevations, in southwestern grasslands. First, they happen less often. Second, although germination may happen early, the plants do not reach maturity until later in the year, after the arrival of the monsoon.

The forbs certainly had a surprise for us that summer of 2001, but it was not the first and it will not be the last. Each year it seems as if one or a few of them becomes common, though usu-

ally they do not dominate as did the asters of 2001. Most of the time we cannot even guess what environmental events might have triggered a particular species to bloom in profusion one year and then be scarcely visible the next.

If grasses are the dominant, stolid citizens of the Sonoita Plain, then forbs are the ephemeral and elusive teases. They also are major providers of diversity, whether one chooses to quantify it numerically, spatially, temporally, entomologically, or even chemically.

Biologists properly describe the Sonoita Valley as a grassland, because in most years the grass species are the most abundant form of vegetation across the landscape. Yet even in ordinary years when the forbs lay low, they are the species that dominate

Antelope horns milkweed

plant variety. Botanists have documented over 500 species of plants on the Research Ranch, and more are being discovered every year. So far, fewer than 90 of these are grasses, while more than 350 of them are forbs. Approximately the same ratio must hold for the valley as a whole, and likely for most of the world's grasslands as well. Describing the Sonoita Plain in terms of grasses alone tells only one small part of the story.

Most grasses are long-lived plants that compete relatively well for space and sunlight and nutrients. By contrast, many of the forbs have evolved to take advantage of disturbance, to seize the day when fire or grazing or drought creates temporary openings in the grassland. Usually it is only a matter of time before the grasses are able to reassert themselves, but meanwhile the forbs

have had a chance to drop their seeds into the soil, where they lie dormant but alive, awaiting the next disturbance. The fact that so many different kinds of forbs are pursuing this opportunistic strategy says something about the frequency and variety of natural disturbances in grasslands.

Another difference between grasses and forbs is how widely they are distributed. Nearly all the common grasses in the Sonoita Valley range well down into Mexico, and many of them extend far to the north as well—up into the central Great Plains as far as Canada. Many of the forbs are relatively provincial by comparison. As a result, forbs make an ever-increasing contribution to the biodiversity of grasslands, as the scale of comparison expands from the local to the regional to the continental. In contemporary sociological terms, grasses are the abundant franchise restaurants and big-box stores that look the same from Calgary to Tucson. Forbs are the one-of-a-kind mom-and-pop outlets that compete relatively poorly with the bigger operations but make local places distinctive and interesting wherever and whenever they can find a niche to fill and a place to hang on.

For reasons that are not entirely clear, forbs have evolved attributes that make them more important than grasses to a wide variety of insects. This means that forbs make a contribution to grassland biodiversity that goes well beyond their own numbers.

The first thing about forbs is that they frequently defend themselves chemically against attacks by herbivorous animals, while grasses rarely do so. That is why many forbs are poisonous, and why they have a bad reputation among ranchers. Many herbivorous insects have developed resistance to these chemical poisons, being involved as they are in evolutionary contests between predator and prey (see chapter four). However, the variety of chemical defenses mobilized by the forbs is so great that a particular insect cannot begin to evolve a tolerance for all of them. The end result is that most grassland (forbland?) herbivorous insects have rather specialized diets, and this in turn leaves room for a wide variety of them to coexist without getting in each other's way. This specialization even extends up the food chain to grassland predators, because many of the herbaceous insects have evolved ways of storing the forb poisons in their own bodies as a means of defending themselves against their enemies.

The second thing about forbs and diversity is that the great majority of them make flowers that are pollinated by animals, while grass pollen is carried from one plant to the next by wind. Much of the species variety of bees, butterflies, moths, and hum-mingbirds in the Sonoita Valley is directly attributable to the forbs that provide them nectar and pollen in exchange for the favor of sexual reproduction. An animal visit works to the plant's advantage only if its pollen (sperm) is delivered to another flower of the same species. This coevolution leads to specialized plant-pollinator relationships and, again, to an increased variety of pollinating animals.

Working against overspecialization in plant-pollinator relationships is the risk to a plant that any particular animal species might be scarce or absent at times, and a similar risk to the animal should its food source disappear. What evolves in most cases is a compromise, and some general rather than absolute patterns result. Thus the flowers of moth-pollinated plants usually open at night and have conspicuous white flowers. Hummingbird-pollinated flowers are open during the day and produce copious nectar in deep tubes that most insects cannot reach. These flowers have little or no odor because hummingbirds have a poor sense of smell. Hummingbird flowers frequently are red, although the reason for this remains unclear since the birds can see a wide variety of colors. Bees are relatively small, see best at the violet end of the color spectrum, and are good at detecting odors. Many bee-pollinated forbs produce sweet-smelling nectar in purple flowers that may have one petal modified as a landing platform.

In a wet year, the Sonoita Plain in late summer and fall will be a grassy green carpet, but the carpet will be interspersed with a patchwork of yellow and red and white and purple because of the forbs. At *their* aesthetic best, the grasses bring order and verdure to the valley, as they wave in tidy unison before the wind. At their aesthetic best, the forbs are an iconoclastic, multicolored mess, without which the valley would be a much less interesting place. The contrast is rather like that of university professors' offices, some of which resemble obsessively manicured lawns, while others appear to have experienced some sort of accidental explosion. Our own offices happen to come in these two extreme forms. We have not yet seen the office of our photographer colleague, but we have a suspicion.

Draw, looking west from East Mesa, late fall

WE NOTED EARLIER that grazing by large hooved mammals is a major biological force shaping the character of most grasslands. Lately in the West most of those large grazers have been ours, and in fact humans have pretty much taken over as the premier grassland mammal. That has been true in the Old World for much longer than the New, but today humans dominate the Sonoita Valley just as much as they do the savannas of East Africa or the steppes of Asia.

Given our collective history as a species that both evolved in and remains dependent on grasslands, there is not much point in thinking about grassland ecology as somehow separate from our own. In fact, it has been a struggle leaving humans out of the first two parts of this book, and the reader will note that we have not fully succeeded. But now it is time to stop any such pretext and to talk about our historic place in the grasslands and savannas of the Sonoita Valley, and what we are doing now, and what it might be like in the future.

This section comprises five chapters. In the first (chapter fifteen), we briefly review the history of the earliest human occupation of the Sonoita Valley, including some things about how those first people lived, and the environmental imprint they might have left behind. In chapter sixteen, we attempt to reconstruct the Sonoita Valley in the first half of the twentieth century, as described by those old-timers who are still around to tell us what it was like when ranching was the predominant human enterprise. Things are changing today, but the ranching legacy has left its mark, both ecologically and culturally. It is one of many things that continue to make the valley an interesting place to live. Another is our neighbor to the south. One cannot understand and fully appreciate either the ecology or the human history of the Sonoita Valley without considering its geographical and cultural proximity to Mexico. That is the subject of chapter seventeen.

The first Americans, and then the Hispanic and Anglo ranchers, all changed the landscape and ecology of the Sonoita Valley but probably not as dramatically as those of us who are moving in today, if only because of our sheer numbers. What will the Sonoita Valley look like in the future? How many of the old ranches will give way to subdivisions? Can we afford to leave room for the uncluttered landscape and biological diversity that attracted many of us here in the first place? These are the subjects of the last two chapters of our book.

A CIRCLE OF STONES was long ago laid out on a low bench above the junction of Post and O'Donnell Canyons, near the present headquarters on the Research Ranch. The stones are not conspicuous when the grass is tall, but they stood out after the Ryan Fire in April of 2002. The circle is perhaps thirty yards across. The stones are partly buried, some clearly set on edge, spaced two or three feet apart. Bits of broken pottery are scattered around inside the circle, some with black or burnt-orange designs. There are some arrowheads and spear points as well. Most of them are broken or incomplete.

Who made the circle of stones, and when? What was its purpose, and why was it laid out in this particular place? We do not know the answers to these questions, but we have been told that these sorts of circles marked traditional living places for the first people of the Sonoita Valley. We have found one other stone circle on the Research Ranch. It is smaller than the one by headquarters, but its setting is similar—next to a wash but not in it, and with a good view. These would be the best sites in which to live: near water essential for crops and attractive to game but away from the danger of floods and the worst of the mosquitoes and diamond-backed rattlesnakes. It cannot be a coincidence that all the present human habitations on the Research Ranch are in the same sorts of places.

The human legacy of the Sonoita Valley is brief, probably dating back no more than ten or twelve thousand years. Yet it must have left a mark. To some uncertain degree, millennia of prior human occupation had shaped the ecosystems that Coronado first saw in 1540. Given the ecological diversity and magnificence of the region in the twenty-first century, this might give us hope for the future of the valley under a continuing human presence. But what *were* the consequences of those earlier human occupations?

The first people to occupy southeastern Arizona were the Clovis big-game hunters, so named by archaeologists for the characteristic projectile points (initially discovered at sites near the present-day Clovis, New Mexico) that they used to hunt large mammals. The Clovis people arrived in the region approximately eleven thousand years ago, and disappeared about a thousand years later. They were succeeded by people of the Cochise Culture, who in turn were followed by the Hohokam, who may have been direct descendants of the Cochise or who may have been new immigrants from what is now Mexico. Present-day Pima and Tohono O'odham peoples of central and southern Arizona and northern Sonora likewise may be directly descended from the Hohokam or may have replaced them.

While many details of this cultural history remain unclear, the ecological trajectory seems to be better understood. In the earliest of Cochise times (8500 BC), the people lived in small nomadic groups, hunting small game and collecting wild plant foods. By 2500 BC, they had begun to develop agriculture and to be more sedentary. By the time of the first Spanish contact, the native peoples lived in villages with the remnants of sophisticated irrigation systems. They grew crops such as agave, corn, beans, and squash, while continuing to hunt small game and to gather wild plant foods.

By the 1690s, the spread of Old World diseases and southward invasion by the Apaches had taken a heavy toll on the original peoples of southeastern Arizona, complicating any assessment

After the monsoon rains: overlooking O'Donnell Canyon toward the Mustangs

of their prehistoric numbers or the ecological legacy they left on the land. Certainly it had to have been modest, compared to the eventual impacts of Anglos and their livestock and mines in the late 1800s.

Or was it?

Amerindian activities that could have affected the grasslands and savannas of the Sonoita Valley include intentional and accidental burning, manipulating riparian ecosystems for crop introductions and irrigation, food-plant gathering, fuelwood cutting, and hunting. Among all these, the impacts of hunting remain the most controversial and perhaps the most significant.

The fossil record leaves no doubt that sizeable populations of large herbivores—including bison, horses, camels, mammoths, and ground sloths—existed in southeastern Arizona 15,000 years ago but are now extinct. Perhaps they had a controlling influence on those prehistoric grasslands the way domestic grazers do today. One powerful and provocative theory contends that the Clovis people exterminated many of those large mammals about 10,000 years ago, easily hunting them to extinction because they had evolved without fear of humans. It is only one step from there to argue that the introduction of cattle and horses and sheep merely rectified that earlier extermination. However, one important distinction must be made: whereas all of these modern herbivores are grazers that feed on grass by choice, some of their Pleistocene counterparts were browsers that ate woody plants. Therefore, the early mammals may have sustained a balance between shrubland and grassland, but domestic grazers handicap only the grasses. The one conceivable reason to introduce another exotic species into Arizona might be to import some sort of large (and tractable) shrub-browsing mammal.

It would be an understatement to say that the theory of human-caused extinctions is controversial, contending as it does that Native American peoples hunted much of North America's large mammal fauna out of existence. Yet this idea is supported by some evidence, especially the fact that similar extinctions appear to have occurred elsewhere in the world coincident with initial human colonizations. If Amerindian peoples did drive some large mammals to extinction, this in no way distinguishes them from any other human populations migrating to new lands. Such extinctions may be inevitable, because prey have insufficient time to evolve defensive or evasive behaviors when they first encounter the world's premier predator: *Homo sapiens.*

The first humans also brought fire to the Sonoita Valley, increasing the frequency and variety of seasons when its grasslands and savannas burned. The earliest written records suggest that the region was far less wooded when first seen by Spanish explorers than it is today. The subsequent spread of trees and shrubs into formerly open grasslands is attributed mainly to reduction in fire fuels eaten by livestock, but it also may have resulted from colonization by fire-wary Europeans who were naïve about the role fire plays in maintaining grasslands as such.

The Europeans who first set eyes on the Sonoita Valley may have found a landscape with more fire and fewer large mammals than would have been the case if they had been the first humans ever in the area. Some of the open-water ecosystems probably had been altered for irrigation, although nothing like the extent to which they would be modified in subsequent centuries.

From the standpoint of conserving contemporary biological diversity, it does not much matter whether humans caused some large mammals to go extinct at the close of the last ice age. We know that many native species of plants and animals in the valley thrive in the presence of large mammalian herbivores, and just as many clearly do not. The same holds for species that need landscapes either burned or unburned. Providing ecological and evolutionary opportunities for all of these species should be the priority. The future of plants and animals that prefer grazed landscapes is secure, as long as there are ranches in the valley. Places without livestock are at least as important because only these can provide space for species intolerant of grazing or those dependent upon fire.

Most but probably not all of the plants and animals that encountered the first humans in the Sonoita Valley survived long enough to greet the first Europeans as well. Most but not all of those are still here today, although one cannot help but miss the Mexican wolf, the Colorado pikeminnow, and, for that matter, nearly all traces of the first Americans themselves. One can only hope that some of their genes prospered in the veins of more recent settlers of the valley and their descendants. Meanwhile, the life-sustaining ecosystems of the Sonoita Valley continue to function, as neither the first nor the most recent human immigrants have pushed them too far. At least, not yet.

THE SONOITA VALLEY is experiencing an influx of in-migrants, some of them retired people who grew up in small towns and on farms of more eastern places, sought their fortunes in America's cities, and then chose to settle here for the next stage of life. Many of these new residents have an interest in human as well as natural history, and they wish to ground themselves in these particular aspects of the valley, perhaps so they will come to feel more a part of the place. This is a good thing, because attachment and immersion are critical first steps toward informed concern for the landscape and its living things.

Archaeologists and anthropologists can tell us about the first humans who lived in the valley (see chapter fifteen), and a good historical record can be found of the life and probable ecological impacts of the early Hispanic and Anglo ranchers and their livestock. But the more recent past is one that we can understand better, because people still live here who can describe it, in ways that are especially poignant for those originally from other parts of rural America. And Hollywood, of all places, has provided some fine visual images.

If you are too busy to come to the Sonoita Valley in person or if you would like to see what it looked like fifty years ago, we recommend renting the right set of old movies. From an ecological perspective, the most startling filming event in the Sonoita Valley was *Oklahoma!* (1955). The central location for that musical was downtown Elgin. And there, in the background, are the Huachuca Mountains. Native Okies have assured us that nothing in their state looks anything like the Huachuca Mountains. Two other unusual landscapes featured in *Oklahoma!* are a peach orchard and a cornfield. The producers imported corn plants individually in pots and set them out in rows to look like the real thing.

A number of classic old westerns and other sorts of movies also were filmed in the Sonoita Valley, and the visual entertainment industry continues to come around. Here is a partial list: *Red River* (1948), *Winchester '73* (1950), *The Last Train from Gun Hill* (1957), *Gunfight at the OK Corral* (1957), and, more recently, *A Star Is Born* (remake, 1976), *Red River* (remake, 1988), and *Tin Cup* (1996). This is only a sample, but viewed in sequence these films reveal how much easier it was back in the 1940s and 1950s to make westerns with their traditional panoramic shots, without the unwanted intrusions of roads, automobiles, and power lines that weren't supposed to be there in the nineteenth century.

In the real world, the village of Elgin was the hub of the Sonoita Valley for the first decades of the twentieth century, with a grocery store, a post office, and a school that served the local ranching community. Sonoita was a lesser place, until the arrival of automobiles favored a town that happened to lie at the junction of two major highways over one that did not. Then Sonoita got the school, the post office, and most of the businesses, and things became relatively quiet in Elgin.

Other small settlements in the Sonoita Valley faded away almost completely after the closure of the mines and the railroad, partly because of the centralization of services made possible by modern transportation. One example is a place called Canelo, on Turkey Creek south of the Research Ranch, which still appears on some maps. Two features identify Canelo. The first is a U.S. Forest Service ranger station. The second is a beautiful old school

Old Elgin School

building, a privately owned and meticulously preserved adobe structure. Some people will tell you they still live in Canelo, but it is a place without a zip code.

An old-timers' story tells of the first teacher at Elgin School. A $3,500 territorial bond passed in 1911 provided money for the building. To complement the bond money, the owner of the Elgin store gave four acres of land upon which the school was built, and it opened in 1912. The first teacher lived some distance away, and she had a baby. Each school day she hitched her horse to the buggy, set the baby on the seat beside her, and passed through a half-dozen gates coming and going. At each gate, she'd get out of the buggy, set the baby on the ground, open the gate, drive the buggy through, pick up the baby and shut the gate,

reload the baby, and continue on. Anyone familiar with horses knows why she would not leave her baby alone in the buggy.

The earliest Elgin pupils varied in age from five to twenty-one years, and it was the first formal educational opportunity for nearly all of them. Eventually a modest home was built beside the three-room schoolhouse so that the teacher could live on site. Elgin School had a small but steady enrollment. Children of all abilities and racial backgrounds were "mainstreamed" from the very beginning—a policy ahead of its time. There were only twenty-three students in 1952, but by the late 1970s enrollment had increased to over seventy, and the school employed three teachers. Temporary buildings were constructed. In the 1980s the first bond issue for a new Elgin School was put forth, but it failed. A subsequent one passed, and students and teachers moved into the new Elgin School, which is closer to Sonoita than to Elgin, in the fall of 1992. To us, the new school has that standard institutional facade that makes it look more like a prison than a place of learning. But a tradition of teaching excellence continues for the many fortunate students who are served at present by numerous fine teachers and staff.

The Elgin Post Office was established in 1910, two years before Arizona statehood. It was adjacent to the Elgin store, and it continued to function both for postal services and as a communication hub for the area until the early 1980s. Unique services provided by the old Elgin Post Office included passing messages when the phones were out and (this actually happened to us)

rewrapping holiday packages if the postmaster deemed them unfit for mailing. Over the door of the grocery store–post office building hung a sign that read: "Elgin, Arizona. Where the sun shines and the wind blows." The sign is gone, but the saying will always be true.

Locals temporarily stalled the demise of the Elgin Post Office by circulating a strongly endorsed petition in 1978, but the post office closed shortly thereafter. Afterward, the residents of Elgin and its vicinity got their mail from a bank of metal boxes, served by rural delivery. The Sonoita Post Office remains the mail distribution center for the valley. It is an intimate, comfortable place and the focus of much social interchange. Everyone we know appreciates the family that shows up outside the Sonoita Post

Office at regular intervals to sell homemade tamales and flour tortillas. Business remains brisk.

The Elgin grocery store closed in the early 1970s, and at present there are two small places in Sonoita that provide staples plus some specialty items. The old-time clientele were ranch people whose needs included veterinary supplies as well as food. Today's customers are a more varied lot, some of whom have specialized and expensive tastes. This means that next to the cans of chili there may be one or two cans of truffles.

The Sonoita area has more restaurants than churches—a notable difference from most small towns in the rural Midwest. We believe this has little or nothing to do with relative levels of religious devotion in the two regions. The problem back there is that eating out can be taken as evidence that a household lacks a good cook—a social stigma. But that is not the way of Sonoita.

Going out to eat in the Sonoita Valley has been an accepted form of weekend reward for many years, and there have been some very good places to do it. Thirty years ago, the two local restaurants were gathering places for people coming from a fifty-mile radius, mostly on Friday and Saturday nights. The restaurants featured local beef or Mexican food. On weekend nights there was live, loud music, and almost everybody actually danced: babies with papas and grannies, neighbors and couples with each other, even teenagers with their parents. Most little girls learned the Texas Two-Step by standing on top of a gentleman's boots.

Current Sonoita restaurant crowds are larger and drawn from greater geographic as well as cultural distances. They include a mixture of people well dispersed along such continua as urban to rural, Anglo to Hispanic, ex-Marine to ex-hippie, and horseback to motorcycle. The variety of foods is greater, but the beef is still

fine. Out-of-town visitors sometimes have difficulty predicting which of the five or six restaurants will happen to be open on any particular day. This gives us locals a foraging advantage. There seems to be less dancing these days, but eating out in Sonoita remains a very great pleasure.

One has to live in the Sonoita Valley for at least fifty years to qualify for burial in the Black Oak Cemetery, at the northern edge of the Canelo Hills. A friend told us the other day that she now has qualified. She came here to live with her new husband, a World War II soldier who owned a local ranch. She had grown up in a genteel New England setting, and she doubtless was unsettled to find that her new home had neither electricity nor running water. When the young bride suffered a serious bout of homesickness, the soldier bought her a round-trip train ticket back home, with an open return date. She stayed in New England just three days and then returned to the Sonoita Valley for keeps. She continues to enjoy life here and to cope with its challenges. The handsome soldier is gone now, but sometimes she dreams of him, those early days, and monsoons past.

It can take a while to fall in love with the Sonoita Valley, especially if one has arrived from some very different place where the climate is less harsh and the grass is green for more of the year. But once it has come, the love tends to last and to be very strong, even today. We have wondered why, beyond the obvious aspects of landscape and biological diversity.

There seem to be two very important *human* things going on in this valley that are relatively unusual. First, the place has yet to be infected by even one franchise business outlet or one subdivision where all the houses look alike. It has escaped, so far, the spatial homogenization that is sucking the spirit out of many places in America. Even the built Sonoita Valley remains a distinctive *place.*

Second, most old-timers welcome most newcomers here, despite all the usual good reasons why they might be inclined to do otherwise. We have heard this attributed to the profound influences of Mexican culture in Santa Cruz County, where a tradition of hospitality, even or perhaps especially to strangers, prevails. We are not so naïve as to suggest that the region is free of the political rancor and personal jealousies that sometimes get out of hand in small communities where people can get to know one another almost too well. But overall the unusual level of courtesy and warmth rounds some of the corners off our American edginess and makes it easier to spend good times in conversation instead of over-achieving at something more materially profitable. That may be another blessing that comes from Mexico, along with the summer monsoon.

LIKE MOST POLITICAL BOUNDARIES, the border between Arizona and Sonora, Mexico, makes no ecological sense. Most living things in the Sonoita Valley pay it no heed. Many birds that breed in the Rocky Mountains migrate south for the winter. If the food is sufficient in Arizona, they stop here. If it is insufficient, they go on down into Mexico.

A variety of Mexican birds come north only as far as southeastern Arizona, and they are the reason that bird-watching is a popular activity in this part of the world. On the Research Ranch, the grassland birds with a Mexican heritage are the major draw, especially Montezuma quail and Botteri's sparrow. Botanists studying the flora of the Research Ranch have found that it has stronger affinities with Mexico than with the Rocky Mountains, or the Great Plains, or the Great Basin of the United States.

Thirty years ago nearly half the names in the Elgin-Sonoita phone book were Spanish, but this proportion has dropped in recent times. This shift almost certainly is due to the recent in-migration of American retirees, rather than the departure of early settlers or their families. People of Spanish descent owned and operated many of the first ranches in the valley. Some of these properties have passed into Anglo-American hands through commerce and marriage, but the imprint of Spain and Mexico continues to prevail, especially with regard to human habitations. Almost all the residences and their outbuildings show a strong Mexican influence. The presence of a saltbox house in the Sonoita Valley would be as strange as the appearance of a one-story adobe on Cape Cod.

From a biogeographic perspective, southeastern Arizona is part of Mexico. However, a considerable effort is spent to keep people from roaming back and forth across the border. This has not stopped a powerful, ongoing, and mutually beneficial exchange. Legitimate cross-border commerce thrives locally, and it preceded the North American Free-Trade Agreement by more than a century. There are many restrictions about what items from each nation can be brought across the line, but "shopping across the border" is both interesting and profitable—from both directions. Included in this exchange are clothing, art objects, dishes and glassware, cosmetics, and many foods and beverages. Some Sonoita Valley ranchers buy and sell livestock across the border. One common pattern is to purchase calves in Mexico, feed them on Sonoita Valley grass, and then ship them to feedlots.

Some of the oldest forms of cross-border commerce involve native plants. Two examples are bear-grass and acorns from the Emory oak. Plants commonly called "bear-grass" are found from North Carolina to Washington State, and the name refers to all sorts of unrelated species. In the Sonoita Valley, "bear-grass" refers to two plants related to yuccas: *Nolina microcarpa* and the less common *Nolina texana*. In Mexico they are called *palmilla*.

With permits from the U.S. Department of Agriculture, a Mexican family group from the state of Sonora comes each year to two of the large ranches in the Sonoita Valley to harvest the leaves of bear-grass plants, which are used to make heavy brooms. The cutters claim that the brooms are of superior quality to those made from plastic. The Mexicans chop off the leaves with machetes before loading bundles of the harvested leaves onto the backs of burros they bring with them and from there onto their trucks. The cutting takes about a month, with a midterm round-trip home to unload the first half of the harvest. This particular

Border Patrol Station, Sonoita

annual exchange has been going on in the Sonoita Valley for at least fifty years, with no apparent long-term decline in bear-grass, since the plants regrow relatively quickly. However, the bear-grass harvest may be getting too intense elsewhere in the Arizona borderlands, because some of the plant populations seem to be declining.

Emory oaks produce sweet acorns that even humans can eat directly off the trees. Other acorns, such as those from Arizona white oak, must be leached of their tannins and other bitter substances before eating them becomes a sound idea for the human digestive tract. Some people of the Yaqui nation who live in northern Sonora and southeastern Arizona have long made use of Emory acorns. The Yaqui grind them into meal, or chop them up for snacks, or use them in other recipes that call for nuts. Grocers in Nogales, Sonora, sell bags of Emory acorns for human consumption. They have been hand-gathered by individuals who know the best trees in the borderlands for producing sweet, copious acorns. In the past the gatherers marked trees of special merit, but most of these were very old and large individuals that were cut down by people more interested in logs than in food. Students at the Research Ranch are encouraged to use Emory acorns in cooking. Occasionally someone slips in an acorn from an Arizona white oak; this facilitates learning how botanists distinguish between the two.

When we first began our field studies at the Research Ranch in the 1970s, it was not uncommon to encounter small groups of people from Mexico, and from other countries farther south, walking north in search of work. We followed the custom of most local ranchers, to give the travelers food and water, and sometimes clothing, and sometimes a day's wages. Twice someone broke into our house when we were gone for the winter. Once a fleece-lined coat was taken. The other time the visitors took nothing, not even the few dollars we had left on top of the bedroom bureau. We did not feel violated or threatened by these events.

Today things have changed. A large Border Patrol station has been established in Sonoita, and nearly every day a helicopter can be seen or heard overhead. Now the immigrants come by the dozens or by the hundreds. Sometimes they trash the land because of their sheer numbers. Sometimes they start fires. Sometimes drugs are involved, and that is the worst part of the border crossing story. But more often it is simply large numbers of good, desperate people. The Border Patrol agents we have met are good people, too, but they have been asked to do an unpopular and nearly impossible job.

There *are* two sorts of bad guys involved in all of this. First, there are the traders in human cargos, who care not for the people who die of heat and thirst. Second, there are those who rant about illegal immigrants one minute and then wink at (or become) their American employers the next.

The situation of "illegals" is much closer to home for residents of the Sonoita Valley than it is for the average American. There must be some better way to deal with our neighbors to the south than inviting them to share in our bounty, usually by working for us, but only after they have been made to run a gauntlet. The search for solutions to drug running and abused human cargos and hungry families consumes us all.

For centuries a steady exchange of animals and plants and people has passed across the ecologically invisible boundary between Mexico and the United States. It has made the Sonoita Valley a richer place—ecologically, aesthetically, and culturally. That is why border crossing continues to be part of our way of life.

THE DAYS WHEN RANCHERS and their cowboys ruled the Sonoita Plain are over. That is less a bad thing or a good thing than it is a sure thing. We have not made an actual count, but it seems there are about the same number of realtors as ranchers in the valley today, if you define a rancher as somebody who actually makes a complete living raising and selling livestock. Housing developments are now scattered across the valley, and doubtless more will come. The Research Ranch, which used to be a place against which to compare the results of grazing, is in the process of becoming a different sort of ecological control.

"Cows not Condos" reads a bumper sticker that is starting to show up all over the West. It is becoming a conspicuous best-seller, and it is as likely to be attached to a university professor's Volvo as to a rancher's pickup truck. We even saw one on an ancient VW bus chugging across the shrub steppe of eastern Oregon. What is going on that could make allies out of redneck cowboys, tree-hugging environmentalists, and academic nerds? Whatever it is, might that be a good thing all by itself?

As we have noted earlier, livestock grazing has been the principal human land use across the interior American West for the past 150 years. Often there have been serious negative consequences for ecosystem function and for native flora and fauna. Increasingly, however, western ranches are being converted to housing developments to accommodate rapid human population growth. This is not in the least surprising, given the marginal profitability of ranching and the potentially high value of private rangelands as real estate. Two questions are central in the minds of ecologists and others interested in the future of the American West. First, what are the impacts of this major land-use change on the biodiversity of western grasslands and savannas, as well as on the people who live in them? Second, what—if anything—can or should be done about it?

Conversion of rural ranchlands to subdivisions has been termed *exurban* development. It involves interplay between land use and landscape alteration, and it is happening in the Sonoita Valley.

The ascent of landscape ecology as an area of scientific inquiry has clarified that the attributes of biological communities are products of both local forces and regional influences. How we use a particular piece of land is important, but so is the condition of the larger area in which it is embedded. Build enough houses close enough together, then pave much of the rest or turn it into swimming pools, lawns, and golf courses, and we can bid a fond farewell to most native plants and wildlife. But water limitations and the mosaic of public and private land means that most western exurban development is scattered and low density. If the remaining open spaces are released from the controlling influences of livestock grazing, are the net environmental effects negative or positive?

The cows versus condos debate rose to prominence with publications in the journal *Conservation Biology* in the mid 1990s that emphasized the negative effects of livestock grazing. These articles provoked strong responses, mostly from ranchers and from scientists at universities with schools of agriculture. These individuals and organizations asserted that the case against grazing was overstated and not supported by adequate study, and that it failed to account for habitat lost to development if and when ranchers were forced out of business and off the land. On the opposite side were those who suggested that postgrazing recovery

Overview of the Sonoita Valley

of the remaining lands would more than offset the habitat lost to development.

The "cows versus condos" debate continues unresolved for at least two reasons. First, in certain ways it is a false dichotomy and a set of nonexistent choices, because some level of western development is inevitable. Furthermore, many of the open spaces in developments will continue to be grazed when landowners keep livestock (especially horses) on their new "ranchettes." The controversy also continues to boil because few data have yet been gathered quantifying the independent and interactive effects of livestock grazing versus exurban development. One reason the "cows versus condos" debate has been strident is that it has been better fueled by a volatile mixture of opinion and emotion than it has been enlightened by information.

Many scientific studies already have described the impacts of landscape alteration on biodiversity, including changes resulting from urban and suburban development. However, much of this information is not directly applicable to the situation in the Sonoita Valley or elsewhere in the West, for the following two reasons.

First, the great majority of studies to date have focused on alteration of forested ecosystems that once were relatively uniform geographically, rather than on the open and naturally heterogeneous landscapes that characterized much of the American West even before development. It is altogether possible that wild animals in the Sonoita Valley are better prepared than their eastern and midwestern siblings to cope with landscape alterations resulting from human activity, because they evolved in places that were highly fragmented to begin with. But we must be careful not to overstate this case, because a mosaic of native trees, shrubs, and grasses certainly is not the same thing as a mixture of houses, shopping centers, and remnant natural landscapes.

Second, environmental scientists mostly have studied the ecological impacts of development in large urban metropolitan areas, the open spaces embedded in or adjacent to them, and the resulting urban gradients. Recent examples include long-term investigations around Los Angeles, Chicago, Seattle, Baltimore, and Phoenix. From these projects we have learned much about how biodiversity might best be protected around our cities. But the lessons are likely to transfer only marginally, if at all, to someplace like the Sonoita Valley.

Environmental biologists are only now beginning to study the ecological consequences of exurban development of former ranchlands in the American West. It is too early to make generalizations, but the results may depend on whether the particular grassland involved had an evolutionary association with bison. For example, recent work at the western edge of the Great Plains in Colorado suggests that converting cattle ranches into rural housing developments, or even ungrazed open spaces, has mostly negative impacts on native grassland birds and vegetation. These formerly uninterrupted grasslands may prove to be among the most sensitive to exurban landscape conversions, whereas domestic livestock impart something like the habitat structure that native grazers once sustained.

The story may be somewhat different in the Sonoita Valley, where grassland, mesquite, and oak form a naturally complex mosaic and where bison have been absent for at least the past ten thousand years. In 2001 we initiated a long-term study comparing biological diversity in parts of the valley that are grazed, or exurbanized, or both, or neither. In the latter category, the Research

Sideoats grama

Ranch serves as a new sort of ecological control. Thanks to the cooperation of the Bureau of Land Management, and with the help of many of our neighbors, we have begun to sample plants, insects, birds, and mammals on fifty-three permanent plots scattered across the valley. We have been gratified by the eagerness and enthusiasm shown by all those willing to let us nose around on their properties.

Our preliminary surveys of birds in the Sonoita area suggest that exurban development may not be entirely bad news, at least at present housing densities. Mourning doves, white-winged doves, scaled quail, and Gambel's quail seem to be more common around the developments, probably because of the relative abundance of water to drink. Say's phoebes, barn swallows, and curve-

billed thrashers like it because of the covered porches and ramadas and shrubs in which to build nests. Mexican jays and Chihuahuan ravens like it for the handouts. Even some of the true grassland birds, such as Botteri's and grasshopper sparrows, are surprisingly common in exurbanized landscapes where good grass cover remains. This may be especially true in the dry seasons, when a yard with a small pool of water may represent a true oasis.

As with everything else we have learned about the Sonoita Valley, the birds seem to be telling us about the importance of variety and diversity in habitat, in landscape, and in land use. We are grateful to those largely anonymous heroes in the Bureau of Land Management and elsewhere who had the vision to trade for the Empire Ranch and to build the Las Cienegas National Conservation Area, to keep at least some of the valley available to those species requiring the wide-open spaces. We applaud the Nature Conservancy for its policy throughout the West of working with ranchers to help them find ways to hang onto their land, when that is what they want to do. We are grateful to the ranchers on the Sonoita Plain who have so far kept their lands intact. And of course we thank the National Audubon Society and the Appleton family for providing a control area. Yet much more than a nod also goes to the developers who have tried to do it right, and especially to our fellow exurbanites who have cared for their land in ways that help sustain the plants and wildlife. So far, it seems to be working.

Certainly an ecological threshold exists, some level of exurban housing density at which natural ecosystems of the Sonoita Valley will start to shut down and the native flora and fauna will start to disappear. The list of threats is obvious: the spread and introduction of nonnative vegetation, too many domestic animals, too many wells, declining air quality, noise and light pollution, overuse of pesticides, and landscape fragmentation. By comparing parts of the valley that support different densities and arrangements of housing, and different sorts of land uses, we should be able to learn where along the developmental continuum these ecological thresholds lie, while there is still time to make a plan.

ARIZONA STATE HIGHWAY 82 starts just outside
Tombstone and ends some sixty-six miles to the southwest, at the border town of Nogales. Highway 83 begins in the low desert east of Tucson, climbs south
into the Sonoita Valley, passes over the Canelo
Hills, and terminates very near the point where Coronado left
Old Mexico on his ride up the valley of the San Pedro River in
1540. Highways 82 and 83 meet only once, at an intersection un-
officially called the Sonoita Crossroads. This junction has been
a hub of human activity in the valley for better than a century.
Today the Sonoita Crossroads is both a place and a point in
time. Nearly all residents wonder what it will look like for their
children and grandchildren.

A citizens' group called the Sonoita Crossroads Community
Forum has adopted a plan for development in the valley, which
was extensively vetted at public meetings. The support was
generally positive, but implementation of the plan will be a
long and complex process. To be effective, it must involve
some limits to growth. This is a tough, complicated, tedious
business. It flies in the face of some very deep convictions in
this country about individual property rights. It is an easy
thing to lose sleep over, because at some point it means
saying to somebody perfectly earnest and moral, "We're
sorry, but you and your family just can't move here." Those
individuals working on a plan for the valley certainly are
aware of the pain involved. We admire them for their courage
and conviction.

What should be the role of the Research Ranch as decisions
are being made about the future of the Sonoita Valley? For inspi-
ration, we turn to two of our environmental heroes, Joseph

Grinnell and Annie Alexander. Together they conceived,
endowed, and built the Museum of Vertebrate Zoology (MVZ)
at the University of California in Berkeley, starting in the
early 1900s. This was no ordinary museum of its day, although
it did end up housing a fine collection of vertebrate animals.
It was a research museum, without public displays. What
made MVZ distinctive were its goals and its methods of
curating information. Almost every specimen of bird, mammal,
reptile, or amphibian was linked by a number to a field notebook
of the zoologist who had collected it. In that notebook the
collector provided details about the place where it had been
found. There also was an excellent photographic record, again
referenced by number to the specimens. What all this meant
was that ecologists and evolutionary biologists could use MVZ
to learn far more than just what an animal looked like. They
also could learn what the land looked like when it had lived
there.

The museum has been an invaluable facility for basic
research, but Joseph Grinnell and Annie Alexander also had
something else in mind. They foresaw that California was a
state destined for something very big, in terms of the numbers
of people who eventually would come there and decide it was
too nice to leave. They understood that the natural world of
their state was due for change, although perhaps even they
could not have imagined just how much. The MVZ collections
were to be a record of what California looked like before this
happened and before the places in which its animals had evolved
were substantially altered. Most critically, they hoped this information would inspire efforts to conserve sufficient natural areas
in California, such that most of its extraordinary biological

Sonoita Crossroads from SR 82

diversity would survive. We hope that, on a very small scale, the record of the Research Ranch and other treasured places we have studied in the Sonoita Valley might serve this purpose in southeastern Arizona.

The Sonoita Valley is one of those Last Best Places, like all of California used to be and most of Montana remains today. In terms of distance from the environmental precipice, the grasslands and oak savannas of southeastern Arizona lie somewhere in between Montana and California, but they are moving toward California. Like these other places, the Sonoita Valley is at risk of falling victim to its own beauty and wonder. The very things that attracted most of us here in the first place are to some inevitable degree put at risk by our collective decision to move in.

The last thing any of us should do about this is to point fingers. As we have noted elsewhere, those environmental issues that present the greatest ethical and strategic dilemmas are those for which most of us are about equally at fault. It is easy to single out an environmental bad guy; it is much less easy when the bad guy turns out to be as much me as you. Human population growth in the Sonoita Valley is not the fault of greedy ranchers or realtors or developers. It is the fault of newcomers like Carl and Jane Bock, and Stephen and Karen Strom, deciding for very good reasons that this is a terrific place to live.

Conserving biological diversity in the Sonoita Valley is a special kind of environmental challenge. It is a place where

Sonoita Post Office

SR 82, east of Sonoita Crossroads

ranchers and environmentalists and exurbanites will have no trouble finding common ground, but they will have trouble finding a common enemy. There *will* be some bad guys at the margins, those get-rich-quick vultures circling around any boomtown whose only goals are to take the money and run. They deserve to be chased out of the valley, and it almost certainly will happen. That leaves the rest of us doing our strategic and ethical best to make some very, very hard decisions. Just how many homes should there be in the valley, on what sized lots, and in what configuration? How many shops and restaurants and other businesses will that require? How much water is in the ground, and how many people can live off it sustainably? Exactly where are those thresholds of development beyond which the grasslands and savannas will start to fall apart?

Debating about what is the most "natural" in nature is an interesting intellectual exercise, but it has little to do with taking care of biological diversity in the real world. Humans have dominated so much of Earth for so long, and especially its grasslands and savannas, that we have no idea what it would be like without us. The point of conservation in the Sonoita Valley is not to preserve some sort of wilderness that probably never existed; it is to make room at the table for other grassland species that call it home in addition to ourselves, wherever and whenever that is possible. This should be seen as largely selfish behavior. Given our numbers and our needs, we cannot hope to protect all grasslands everywhere, much less (alas) to save every grassland species. But the valley would be diminished without the grasses and the oaks, just as it would be without Botteri's sparrows, Mojave rattlesnakes, pronghorn, and horses. Follow any other worldview to its logical outcome, and you end up with a landscape as barren as the surface of Mars or the Moon.

Those three universal reasons to protect biological diversity are as applicable on the Sonoita Plain as they are anywhere in the world. We need it, we like it, and it is the right thing to do.

APPENDIX 1 — Common and Scientific Names of Plants and Animals

This list includes species in the Sonoita Valley that are mentioned in the text.

Grasses

blue grama . . . . *Bouteloua gracilis*
Boer lovegrass . . . . *Eragrostis curvula* var. *conferta*
cane beardgrass . . . . *Bothriochloa barbinodis*
curly-mesquite. . . . . *Hilaria belangeri*
hairy grama . . . . *Bouteloua hirsuta*
Lehmann lovegrass . . . . *Eragrostis lehmanniana*
plains lovegrass . . . . *Eragrostis intermedia*
sacaton . . . . *Sporobolus wrightii*
sideoats grama. . . . . *Bouteloua curtipendula*
sprucetop grama . . . . *Bouteloua chondrosioides*
tanglehead. . . . . *Heteropogon contortus*
Texas bluestem . . . . *Schizachyrium cirratus*
three-awn grasses. . . . . *Aristida* spp.
vine-mesquite . . . . *Panicum obtusum*
wolftail . . . . *Lycurus phleoides*

Forbs

antelope horns milkweed. . . . . *Asclepias asperula*
Arizona mariposa lily. . . . . *Calochortus ambiguus*
cudweed . . . . *Gnaphalium canescens*
duckweed . . . . *Lemna* sp.
goldeneye . . . . *Viguiera dentata*
jimsonweed . . . . *Datura wrightii*
Mexican gold-poppy . . . . *Eschscholtzia mexicana*
Pricklepoppy . . . . *Argemone pleiacantha*
purple aster . . . . *Machaeranthera tagetina*
yellow aster . . . . *Machaeranthera gracilis*

Trees, Shrubs, and Succulents

alligator juniper. . . . . *Juniperus deppeana*

Arizona sycamore . . . . *Platanus wrightii*
Arizona walnut . . . . *Juglans major*
Arizona white oak . . . . *Quercus arizonica*
bear-grass. *Nolina microcarpa*
Emory oak. . . . . *Quercus emoryi*
Fremont cottonwood. . . . . *Populus fremontii*
Goodding willow. . . . . *Salix gooddingii*
Huachuca agave. . . . . *Agave parryi* var. *huachucensis*
mesquite . . . . *Prosopis velutina*
mountain mahogany . . . . *Cercocarpus montanus*
one-seed juniper . . . . *Juniperus monosperma*
Palmer agave (lechuguilla) . . . . *Agave palmeri*
rainbow cactus. . . . . *Echinocereus rigidissimus*
Stansbury cliff rose . . . . *Purshia stansburiana*
velvet ash. *Fraxinus velutina*
yerba-de-pasmo . . . . *Baccharis pteronioides*
yucca. . . . . *Yucca elata* and *Yucca schottii*

Insects

backswimmer . . . . *Notonecta* sp.
barberpole grasshopper . . . . *Dactylotum variegatum*
panther grasshopper . . . . *Poecillotettix pantherinus*
water strider . . . . *Geris remigis*

Fishes

Colorado pikeminnow . . . . *Ptychocheilus lucius*

Amphibians and Reptiles

black-tailed rattlesnake . . . . *Crotalus molossus*
bunchgrass lizard. . . . . *Sceloporus slevini*
Chiricahua leopard frog. . . . . *Rana chiricahuensis*

gopher snake . . . . *Pituophis catenifer*
Mexican garter snake . . . . *Thamnophis eques*
Mojave rattlesnake . . . . *Crotalus scutulatus*
Sonoran whipsnake . . . . *Masticophis bilineatus*
western diamond-backed
    rattlesnake . . . . *Crotalus atrox*

Birds
barn swallow . . . . *Hirundo rustica*
Botteri's sparrow . . . . *Aimophila botterii*
cactus wren . . . . *Campylorhynchus brunneicapillus*
Cassin's sparrow . . . . *Aimophila cassinii*
Chihuahuan raven . . . . *Corvus cryptoleucus*
common snipe . . . . *Gallinago gallinago*
Cooper's hawk . . . . *Accipiter cooperii*
curve-billed thrasher . . . . *Toxostoma curvirostre*
Gambel's quail . . . . *Callipepla gambelii*
grasshopper sparrow . . . . *Ammodramus savannarum*
greater yellowlegs . . . . *Tringa melanoleuca*
horned lark . . . . *Eremophila alpestris*
lark sparrow . . . . *Chondestes grammacus*
Mexican duck (mallard) . . . . *Anas platyrhynchos*
Mexican jay . . . . *Aphelocoma ultramarina*
Montezuma quail . . . . *Cyrtonyx montezumae*
mourning dove . . . . *Zenaida macroura*
northern flicker . . . . *Colaptes auratus*
northern mockingbird . . . . *Mimus polyglottos*
prairie falcon . . . . *Falco mexicanus*
savannah sparrow . . . . *Passerculus sandwichensis*
Say's phoebe . . . . *Sayornis saya*
scaled quail . . . . *Callipepla squamata*
Townsend's solitaire . . . . *Myadestes townsendi*

vesper sparrow . . . . *Pooecetes gramineus*
white-winged dove . . . . *Zenaida asiatica*

Mammals
Arizona cotton rat . . . . *Sigmodon arizonae*
beaver . . . . *Castor canadensis*
collared peccary (javelina) . . . . *Tayassu tajacu*
coyote . . . . *Canis latrans*
deer mouse . . . . *Peromyscus maniculatus*
hispid pocket mouse . . . . *Chaetodipus hispidus*
lesser long-nosed bat . . . . *Leptonycteris curasoae*
Merriam's kangaroo rat . . . . *Dipodomys merriami*
Mexican wolf . . . . *Canis lupus baileyi*
mountain lion . . . . *Felis concolor*
mule deer . . . . *Odocoileus hemionus*
northern pygmy mouse . . . . *Baiomys taylori*
pronghorn . . . . *Antilocapra americana*
rock squirrel . . . . *Spermophilus variegatus*
silky pocket mouse . . . . *Perognathus flavus*
tawny-bellied cotton rat . . . . *Sigmodon fulviventer*
white-tailed deer . . . . *Odocoileus virginianus*
yellow-nosed cotton rat . . . . *Sigmodon ochrognathus*

APPENDIX 2   Visiting the Research Ranch

The primary purposes of the Appleton-Whittell Research Ranch Sanctuary are science and conservation, and there are no regularly scheduled public activities. However, individuals are welcome to visit the property under most circumstances, for personal activities such as bird-watching and hiking.

If you plan to visit, please call in advance at (520) 455-5522 or e-mail researchranch@audubon.org. When you enter the ranch property, follow the signs to headquarters to sign in and to learn which areas might be closed because of current fieldwork. Roads to the sanctuary cross private ranches that otherwise are not open to the public without the landowner's permission.

The sanctuary's Grassland Center is an excellent place for group meetings on topics related to conservation and land use. Occasional workshops and other activities are open to the public; these require advance sign-up.

Visit the sanctuary website (www.audubonresearchranch.org) for information about the flora and fauna, meetings, workshops, and other activities. For general information about the National Audubon Society in Arizona, contact Audubon Arizona at (602) 468-6470 or visit the organization's website (www.audubon.org).

FURTHER READING

There is a very large technical literature on the ecology, paleobiology, and environmental history of southwestern grasslands and savannas. Detailed review of that literature is beyond the scope or intention of this book. However, the following titles include synthetic works and certain other key references on these general topics, as well as texts that focus on the Research Ranch and the Sonoita Valley in particular. In our earlier book, cited below, we included a comprehensive review of technical publications resulting from fieldwork at the Research Ranch.

Bahre, C. J. 1991. *A Legacy of Change: Historic Human Impact on Vegetation in the Arizona Borderlands.* University of Arizona Press, Tucson.

Bock, C. E., and J. H. Bock. 2000. *The View from Bald Hill: Thirty Years in an Arizona Grassland.* University of California Press, Berkeley.

Brown, D. E., and C. H. Lowe (editors). 1983. *Biotic Communities of the Southwest.* General Technical Report RM-78. Rocky Mountain Forest and Range Experiment Station, Fort Collins, Colo.

Byers, J. A. 1997. *American Pronghorn: Social Adaptations and the Ghosts of Predators Past.* University of Chicago Press, Chicago.

Forman, R.T.T. 1995. *Land Mosaics: The Ecology of Landscapes and Regions.* Cambridge University Press, New York.

Gehlbach, F. R. 1981. *Mountain Islands and Desert Seas: A Natural History of the U.S.-Mexico Borderlands.* Texas A & M University Press, College Station.

Hastings, J. R., and R. M. Turner. 1965. *The Changing Mile: An Ecological Study of Vegetation Change with Time in the Lower Mile of an Arid and Semiarid Region.* University of Arizona Press, Tucson.

Humphrey, R. R. 1987. *90 Years and 535 Miles: Vegetation Changes along the Mexican Border.* University of New Mexico Press, Albuquerque.

Jemison, R., and C. Raish. 2000. *Livestock Management in the American Southwest: Ecology, Society, and Economics.* Elsevier, Amsterdam.

Martin, P. S., and R. G. Klein (editors). 1984. *Quaternary Extinctions: A Prehistoric Revolution.* University of Arizona Press, Tucson.

McClaran, M. P., and T. R. Van Devender (editors). 1995. *The Desert Grassland.* University of Arizona Press, Tucson.

McPherson, G. R. 1997. *Ecology and Management of North American Savannas.* University of Arizona Press, Tucson.

National Research Council. 1999. *Perspectives on Biodiversity: Valuing Its Role in an Ever-Changing World.* National Academy Press, Washington, D.C.

Parker, K. F. 1972. *An Illustrated Guide to Arizona Weeds.* University of Arizona Press, Tucson.

Pyne, S. J., P. L. Andrews, and R. D. Laven. 1996. *Introduction to Wildland Fire* (second edition). John Wiley & Sons, New York.

Riebsame, W. E. (general editor), and J. J. Robb (director of cartography). 1997. *Atlas of the New West.* W. W. Norton, New York.

Tellman, B. (editor). 2002. *Invasive Exotic Species in the Sonoran Region.* University of Arizona Press, Tucson.

Turner, R. M., R. H. Webb, J. E. Bowers, and J. R. Hastings. 2003. *The Changing Mile Revisited.* University of Arizona Press, Tucson.

Wilson, E. O. 2002. *The Future of Life.* Alfred A. Knopf, New York.

ABOUT THE AUTHORS

CARL BOCK received his Ph.D. in zoology from the University of California at Berkeley in 1968. He is an emeritus professor of ecology and evolutionary biology at the University of Colorado in Boulder. Carl is an ornithologist who pioneered the use of the National Audubon Society's databases for monitoring the distribution of North American birds.

JANE BOCK received her Ph.D. in botany from the University of California at Berkeley in 1966. She is an emeritus professor of ecology and evolutionary biology at the University of Colorado in Boulder and is on the board of directors for the Center of the American West. She also is an international authority on forensic botany—the use of plant materials in criminal investigations.

The Bocks are grassland ecologists and conservation biologists who have worked from the prairies of South Dakota and Montana to the arid desert grasslands of the Southwest that are the particular focus of this book. They are coauthors of *The View from Bald Hill: Thirty Years in an Arizona Grassland* (2000). They were codirectors of the Research Ranch Sanctuary for the National Audubon Society from 1980 to 1991.

STEPHEN STROM is an astronomer at the National Optical Astronomy Observatory. He received his Ph.D. in astronomy from Harvard University and has held appointments at Harvard, the State University of New York at Stony Brook, and the University of Massachusetts at Amherst, where he served as chair of the Five College Astronomy Department for nearly fourteen years. For the past twenty years, Stephen's research has been focused on studies of forming stars and planetary systems.

Since 1978, Stephen has photographed extensively in the American Southwest. His work has appeared in more than thirty exhibitions throughout the United States and is archived in a number of collections, including the Center for Creative Photography at the University of Arizona and the Mead Museum in Amherst, Massachusetts. His interpretations of landscapes in the Four Corners region accompany Joy Harjo's poems in *Secrets from the Center of the World* (1989).